DAY TRIPS
around
TORONTO

John Barber

FIREFLY BOOKS

DEDICATION
This book is dedicated to all city dwellers who love the
countryside.

ACKNOWLEDGEMENTS
The name of a single author on the cover of this
book does no justice to the broad collaboration that
produced it. Innumerable tourist officials, business
operators, enthusiasts, museum attendants, volunteers
and local tipsters guided the research, providing a
wealth of information and photographs that I did my
best to collate and edit. God bless them all and also
Google Maps. Any errors are my own. Special thanks
to all those at Firefly Books who first recognized the
merit of the project and then did so much to bring a
bare manuscript to life, especially Lionel Koffler, Steve
Cameron and Julie Takasaki. Thanks also to Marijke
Friesen for her fabulous design and Catherine Dorton
for her helpful edits.

A Firefly Book

Published by Firefly Books Ltd. 2018
Copyright © 2018 Firefly Books Ltd.
Text copyright © John Barber 2018
Photographs © as listed on page 237

First printing

Library of Congress Control Number: 2018941770

Library and Archives Canada Cataloguing in
Publication
Barber, John, 1954-, author
     Day trips around Toronto / John Barber.

Includes index.
ISBN 978-1-77085-936-4 (softcover)

1. Toronto Region (Ont.)—Guidebooks.
2. Ontario, Southern—Guidebooks.
3. Guidebooks. I. Title.

FC3097.18.B37 2018   917.13'54104
C2018-902288-4

Published in the United States by
Firefly Books (U.S.) Inc.
P.O. Box 1338, Ellicott Station
Buffalo, New York 14205

Published in Canada by
Firefly Books Ltd.
50 Staples Avenue, Unit 1
Richmond Hill, Ontario L4B 0A7

Cover and interior design: Marijke Friesen
Maps: Bill Syrett, ontariotrailmaps.ca

Printed in Canada

Canadä

We acknowledge the financial support of the
Government of Canada.

DISCLAIMER
This book is for information purposes only. The
authors and publisher have tried their best to ensure
the accuracy of the information in this book. The
conditions of the parks, forests and conservations
areas described in this book may change over time,
and certain businesses or institutions may move or
close. The publisher highly recommends that you check
whether a particular destination is open before you
depart. The author and publisher are not responsible for
any thefts, issues or misfortunes that may arise from the
use of the information in this book.

Table of Contents

INTRODUCTION 5

Humber Valley 14

Happy Valley Forest 19

Sharon Temple 23

Credit River Valley & Caledon 27

The Headwaters 32

Minesing Wetlands & Creemore 36

Orillia Arts & Tarts 40 *Sep 2 '23*

Sainte-Marie among the Hurons, Wye
    Marsh & Discovery Harbour 46

OCT 17 '21

OCT 17 '21 Wasaga Beach 51

Collingwood & Blue Mountain
    Village 55

Kolapore Uplands & Ravenna 60

Flesherton & Beaver Valley 64

FEATURE

The Simcoe Snowbelt 67

Hamilton Art & Architecture 74

Royal Botanical Gardens & the
    Escarpment 79

Hamilton History & Heritage 86

Welland Canal 90

Niagara Falls 93 *Dec 26, '21*

Niagara Region Bike Train Routes 97

Queenston Heights 102

Niagara Wine Region 107

Niagara-on-the-Lake 112 *Dec 26 '21*

Lake Erie's Deep South 118

FEATURE

The Niagara Freedom Trail 123

Oshawa's High Culture 132

Glen Major & Walker Woods 135

Uxbridge Township 139

Lake Scugog 143

Canadian Tire Motorsport Park 147

Ganaraska Forest 151

Port Hope 156 *May 20 '23*

Cobourg 162 *''*

Northumberland County Circuit 166

✓Peterborough 170 *Feb 19 '23*

Lang Pioneer Village 175

Presqu'ile Provincial Park 178 *May 20 '23*

Prince Edward County Wine Tour 182

Prince Edward County Cycling *May 21 '23*
   Routes 185

Great War Flying Museum 200

Halton Parks 203

Guelph 208

African Lion Safari & Galt 213

Paris 216

Six Nations of the Grand River 220

✓Elora 224 *JUN 11, '21*

St. Jacobs 228

Stratford 233

PHOTO CREDITS 237

INDEX 238

FEATURE

GO Transit Cycle Tours 191

Introduction

A persistent vision hung in my mind during the writing of this book: I pictured a young family in the near suburbs of Toronto, parents shaken awake early on a Sunday morning by a pair of rambunctious children who are wondering what they're going to do today. Nothing much comes to mind — the mall beckons, maybe they could run an errand or two. Meanwhile, the kids gravitate toward their screens. By the afternoon, the family settles for a walk in High Park and hot chocolates at Starbucks.

Consider this book to be a kind of intervention: a quick-reference tool to help prevent another wasted day off — in fact, to help make the most of your free days. These pages contain dozens of suggestions for wholesome and affordable day trips in the increasingly attractive countryside surrounding Toronto. Some destinations are well known, others more obscure, but most of them are as easy as a walk in the park. You needn't plan ahead or travel far to reach them. All that's needed is the willingness to think outside the 630-square-kilometre box that is Toronto.

Usually when that willingness appears, cottage country is the destination that first comes to mind. But while cottage country becomes ever more exclusive and suburban, there is a renaissance afoot in the immediate hinterlands of Toronto. It's transforming both the natural and human landscapes and recreating a distinctive identity for the broad area the Haudenosaunee people called "Tkaronto."

This pleasant vision is admittedly hard to see from inside the modern city, where the outward view is blocked by what seems to be interminable urban sprawl. But 70 years of strong conservation legislation, culminating in the Ontario Greenbelt, has massively restored the formerly devastated forests of Toronto's natural borderlands. The urban boundary is now sharply defined, and the country beyond is quickly recovering its former grace. Rivers run clear and cold, and wildlife has returned.

Just as remarkably, picturesque towns and villages once left for dead are now thriving in their new post-industrial roles. Concern for environmental conservation and human heritage have grown together like twins, creating new recreational opportunities and transforming local economies. Thus ancient Tkaronto reappears in modern guise, both as a treasured natural landscape and as a comfortably settled, often intriguing and sometimes delightful human habitat — one to be celebrated and enjoyed.

Tourism in the Toronto region used to mean one thing only: Niagara Falls. Today, the landscape is brimming with opportunities for recreational and cultural experiences. From the internationally prominent theatre festivals in Stratford and Niagara-on-the-Lake to the Bruce Trail, the wineries of Prince Edward County and the beaches of Lake Erie's deep south, hundreds of new attractions throng this once-neglected hinterland.

This book celebrates this new era of Ontario tourism, striving to show the diversity of outings available. Almost all the destinations can be reached within a 90-minute drive from Yonge Street and Highway 401. If a few are a bit farther away, such as the Stratford

One key to a successful day trip outdoors is preparedness. If you make it a habit, the basic necessities will fall easily to hand. Water, sunscreen, insect repellent, snacks and rain gear are essential for any outing, especially with children along. You should also make sure to carry a charged-up cellphone with GPS. Although most of the spots featured here are well marked, it's still easy to get lost. Lastly, if it's cold or wet, nothing is more welcoming than a stash of dry clothes waiting in the car.

Festival or Prince Edward County, that only means they're worth the extra effort (and kilometres). Wherever possible, I've included directions for outings that can be made exclusively on public transit — an increasingly attractive alternative, given today's traffic.

In general, I've favoured the small and quirky over the big and commercial, figuring that Marineland can afford its own promotion but the Hamilton Museum of Steam and Technology is a more modest operation that deserves your attention. Historical monuments, culture and architecture figure large, as does the simple pleasure of strolling around a picturesque town. You'll also find a distinct bias in favour of outdoor experiences. There are two reasons for that. One is that hiking, cycling, skiing and paddling are always the most affordable options for any day trip. The other is that there are just so many opportunities — many little known or overlooked — to enjoy nature on Toronto's doorstep.

This book has been divided into directional chapters with the destinations within each chapter roughly ordered by distance from Toronto. The beginning of each chapter has a detailed road map with select attractions highlighted in red. Although I've featured over 45 headline destinations, each entry also includes suggestions for different options and side trips. If you go rafting on the Grand River near Paris, you'll definitely want to check out that town's unusual cobblestone architecture. If you visit the Canadian Canoe Museum in Peterborough, you really should make time for a leisurely cycle or driving tour along the Otonabee River to Lakefield. My aim is to present constellations of experiences that will more than fill a single day — and perhaps encourage return trips to favourite haunts first discovered in the ensuing pages. I've also included three special entries: the Simcoe Snowbelt, the Niagara Freedom Trail and GO Transit Cycle Tours. Each highlights a particular theme or region and gives more ideas for great day trips away from the city.

Happy touring!

NORTH

Going north is the most Canadian thing a person can do: the annual summer migration to the granite-clad lake country is as certain as anything in nature. Ceaselessly we stream — or more likely crawl — north, willing to accept any indignity in order to sleep overnight in a lakeside suburb that increasingly resembles the one we just left. Lemmings were never more determined, nor more oblivious to the attractions they hurry past as they struggle to fulfill their fate.

This chapter is devoted to the rich recreational experiences to be found on the wayside of the trodden path. Some are obvious and well-known: Wasaga Beach is the classic day-trip alternative to a weekend up north, and the Blue Mountain Resort has transformed Collingwood from a ho-hum ski hill into a major destination overflowing with novel activities and amenities. But others are not obvious at all: the headwaters of the Humber and Credit Rivers, once barren and deforested, are now rich with recreational opportunities, and the historical monuments of Sharon Temple and Sainte-Marie among the Hurons are virtually obligatory.

This is not the quaint and settled country you find in the more southerly reaches of the province. It is the "Land Between" — more rugged, less populated and little noticed on the cottage-country flyways. But you can gain a lot by stopping short.

A handful of destinations in this chapter feature a section called "Bruce Trail Adventures," which highlights special segments of this amazing 900-kilometre trail. Hiking the Bruce is richly rewarding and free for the doing, almost. Before you lace up your hiking boots and embark, you'll definitely need to buy a copy of *The Bruce Trail Reference Maps & Trail Guide*, which you can order online at brucetrail.org, a great resource for learning more about the trail. If you prefer, you can buy individual maps for specific trail sections or get the whole lot in the Bruce Trail app from the App Store or Google Play.

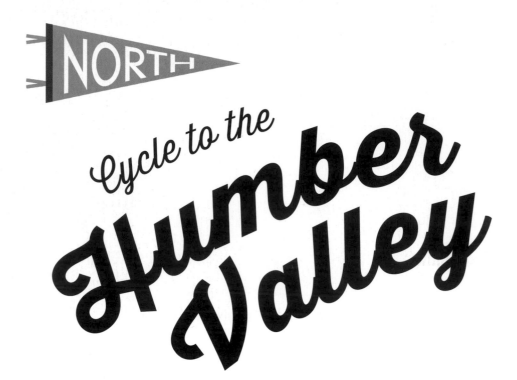

NORTH

Cycle to the

Humber Valley

If there were nominees for best cycling day trips out of Toronto, the list would have to include a summer ride up the Humber Valley to Kleinburg for a visit to the McMichael Canadian Art Collection, a picnic on its sculpture-dotted grounds and a leisurely evening spin back down the valley into the city. The valley is gorgeous all the way north, and the trip exemplifies the best of what the region is becoming while avoiding the worst — i.e., the highways. The river route that gave Toronto its purpose centuries ago is once again a pathway, its headwaters a nexus of trails that spread out like green veins throughout central Ontario.

In addition to great Canadian art, the area is awash with outdoor opportunities, both tame and on the wilder side.

McMichael Canadian Art Collection

The McMichael Canadian Art Collection is an essential destination. Even if you think you've already seen enough of Tom Thomson and the Group of Seven, the McMichael reminds you that you haven't. But it's no mere

museum of an old nationalism. The gallery's programming consistently ventures new connections to contemporary art while maintaining its central preoccupation with the Canadian landscape.

It's also a refreshingly eccentric place, having originated in the romantic vision of its founding couple and grown organically over the years. Its rustic log construction and sweeping valley views pay scant heed to the cool contemporary norm, creating a distinctive personality that has remained intact despite the gallery's subsequent expansion into a well-funded, white-walled institution.

Free public tours are offered for the price of admission. Pack a lunch, eat outdoors and enjoy a walk in the surrounding Humber River forest. Or enjoy the forest view from the floor to-ceiling glass windows of Aura, the gallery's restaurant.

The front entrance of the McMichael Canadian Art Collection.

ARRIVING BY BIKE

If you are adventurous enough to tackle the long journey to McMichael by bike, follow the Humber East Trail north to its terminus, jog east on Steeles and then north on Islington. You can leave Islington 5 kilometres north of Steeles at the Boyd Conservation Area, and from there follow the William Granger Greenway (a gravel path) north to the gallery.

The Toronto-York Spadina Subway Extension to Vaughan Metropolitan Centre at Highway 7 promises easier, albeit far less scenic, bicycle access to the McMichael. The route runs west from Vaughan Metropolitan Centre station, following Portage Parkway, Chancellor Drive and Willis Road to Islington. It's about 11 kilometres one way.

Kleinburg

If you've made it to the McMichael, you are three minutes away from Kleinburg. Back in the day, the village of Kleinburg was a proudly rustic antidote to the smoky city, where locals celebrated the annual distribution of something called binder twine and appointed as beauty queen their young woman most adept in its use, as well as at milking cows and chopping wood. The Binder Twine Festival still takes place every September, attracting tens of thousands to the village for its old-time activities and parade, but otherwise Kleinburg today is almost as slick as Bloor Street, a high-toned shopping district lined with sophisticated restaurants and boutiques. But the historic theme is authentic and carefully tended. Even the Starbucks, located in an 1832 farmhouse trucked in from the nearby countryside, is charming and easily one of the nicest sidewalk cafés in the GTA. A few doors north at 10516 Islington Avenue, the Canadian Heritage Art Company complements the McMichael experience with a specialty in traditional Canadiana.

Conservation Areas

◆ Kortright Centre for Conservation

A 10-minute drive (or 20-minute bike ride) from the McMichael takes you to the Kortright Centre for Conservation. This is a busy place that has instructed untold thousands of local schoolchildren in the ways of nature and sustainable living, becoming ever more relevant as the suburbs spread outward to envelop it. Even if they've been already, your school-age kids will want to visit again. The Kortright is busiest during its annual Sugarbush Maple Syrup Festival, which demon-

RIGHT
Visitors on a guided program at the Kortright Centre for Conservation.

Kleinburg's Starbucks matches the village's charm.

strates the old-fashioned techniques of tapping trees and boiling sap, and it's also popular in the summer for picnics and weddings. Recently added attractions include two houses built to demonstrate green building techniques and the new headquarters of Earth Rangers, a wildlife rescue and education centre.

The centre is located in Woodbridge at 9550 Pine Valley Drive, north of Rutherford Road.

• Albion Hills Conservation Area

The Albion Hills Conservation Area, a 30-minute drive north of Kleinburg, could well be the most popular place of its kind in Ontario, thanks to its proximity to Toronto, its spaciousness and the sheer variety of organized programming it makes available. Mountain bikes and cross-country runners dominate the trails in the summer, while winter attracts the largest number of cross-country skiers in the region. An enormous wading pool and splash pad serve swimmers. A full range of facilities in the chalet, including showers, a snack bar and equipment rentals, make all of it easy.

Despite the occasional crush on a fair-weather weekend, winter or summer, Albion Hills still offers the ideal introduction to outdoor adventure in the Toronto region. It's located off Highway 50, just north of Bolton.

Albion Hills Conservation Area.

◆ Palgrave Forest and Wildlife Area

A few kilometres up the same highway will bring you to the Palgrave Forest and Wildlife Area, an altogether different experience on neighbouring terrain. Relatively undeveloped, with no facilities or entrance fees, it has a fairly large network of cycling, riding and un-groomed ski trails winding amid the hills and ponds. They are now easily navigable thanks to recently installed signage. Otherwise, you're on your own. Parking is available on the west side of Highway 50, just south of the Humber Bridge.

◆ Glen Haffy Conservation Area

Interested in trying your hand at amateur angling? Glen Haffy Conservation Area (at 19245 Airport Road, a 15-minute drive from Palgrave) stocks its ponds and lake with rainbow trout raised from its own fish hatchery. Best of all, you don't need a licence! Equipment, bait and tackle are available for rent onsite.

◆ Hiking the Heritage and Conservation Trails

The easy accessibility of Albion Hills and the Kortright Centre has had the unusual effect of leaving vast acres of the upper Humber Valley relatively untrammelled. Almost all of the valley land between Kleinburg and Palgrave is owned and managed by the Toronto Region Conservation Authority, which is gradually building trails and improving access with the help of local volunteers. There's magic in travelling the ancient route that gave Toronto its name and remains, along these upper stretches, as wild as it ever was.

Two interconnected trail systems follow the upper Humber: the Humber Valley Heritage Trail, upstream from Bolton to Palgrave, and the trails of the Nashville Conservation Reserve, between Bolton and Kleinburg.

Getting There

The Humber Valley trails are easily accessible from a number of road crossings and well documented at humbertrail.org.

To find the Nashville trails, follow Nashville Road west from Kleinburg and turn north on Huntington Road. The trailhead is a few kilometres north at the corner of Huntington and Kirby.

Hike the Happy Valley Forest

If you've ever had a mind to visit an old-growth forest in southern Ontario, forget it: Only traces of the magnificent woodlands that once blanketed these hills remain standing. There are probably more trees older than 120 years in Queen's Park than there are in any of the relatively young forests that have reappeared since the severe scalping Ontario suffered in the 19th century. However, one of the finest and least disturbed of those tracts — and well on its way to becoming true old growth — is located 15 kilometres due north of Canada's Wonderland.

The Goldie Feldman Nature Reserve is a popular entrance to the Happy Valley Forest.

Trilliums carpet the forest in the spring.

160-kilometre length of the Oak Ridges Moraine — itself the largest span of contiguous forest in the settled south of the province. Happy Valley hosts what Nature Ontario describes as "an exceptional array of rare and conservative woodland birds," being one of the few Canadian habitats left for such threatened species as the Hooded Warbler and Acadian Flycatcher." The forest is also home to creek valleys,

Happy Valley Forest

The faster the suburban frontier approaches, the more remarkable the Happy Valley Forest becomes, still largely undisturbed after two centuries of wanton cutting all around it. It is not only the closest real forest to Toronto, it is the most extensive woodland complex along the entire

𝒢𝑒𝓉𝓉𝒾𝓃𝑔 𝒯𝒽𝑒𝓇𝑒

To get to Happy Valley from Toronto, drive north on Highway 400 to King Road (Exit 43), turn west on King and immediately north (right) onto Weston Road. There is an entrance to the Oak Ridges Trail 4 kilometres north, which follows the unopened allowance of the 16th Sideroad west into the forest.

Alternatively, you can drive north on Weston another few kilometres and turn west onto the 17th Sideroad, which leads to another trailhead at the Goldie Feldman Nature Reserve.

To get closest to the heart of the forest, continue north on Highway 400 to the Lloydtown-Aurora Road (Exit 52) and follow it west to the community of Pottageville. Turn south (left) on the 7th Concession Road, which reaches the trailhead at a dead end 2.8 kilometres later.

wooded swamps, kettle ponds and minor wetland areas. A huge range of tree species thrive here, including maples, beech, oak, birch, hemlock and aspen, and all of it is easily visible from the top of a suburban roller coaster.

The best time to visit Happy Valley is in the spring, when cabin fever finally breaks and all Canadians crave the rich smell of unfrozen earth. There is no better place to enjoy the early, brief appearance of what botanists call "spring ephemerals," plants that thrive only in the forest and flower early, before the high canopy closes in and darkens the ground. They include such deep-forest stalwarts as Jack-in-the-pulpit, trout lily, skunk cabbage and, most famously, extensive carpets of trillium. Take a camera and wear your gumboots.

Despite its proximity to the city, the Happy Valley Forest can be challenging to navigate. There is a map and other interpretive material posted at the Goldie Feldman Nature Reserve, a popular starting point for hikes, but no washroom facilities exist in the forest or at the trailheads.

The heat and bugs discourage summer outings, but come September Happy Valley is one of the best places

This red-spotted newt is one of Happy Valley Forest's numerous residents.

in the GTA to experience fall colours. It's almost fun to get lost so close to the city, but ensure you take plenty of water, snacks and a GPS.

Lloydtown

Public-art oddities are not uncommon in these hinterlands, but the flyspeck hamlet of Lloydtown has something nobody else does: a heroic statue memorializing the ragtag band that raised arms against the colonial government in the abortive Rebellion of 1837. Standing tall with a musket in one hand and gesturing with the other hand south, in the direction of the Establishment enemy in Toronto, the Rebel defiantly insists on celebrating a debacle in which the residents of Lloydtown, led by rebel leader Jesse Lloyd, played a leading role. While you are there, take a walking tour through the hilly countryside. The path begins near the Pioneer Cemetery. A less than 15-minute drive from the Happy Valley Forest west along Lloydtown-Aurora Road, Lloydtown is an easy side trip.

The Rebel statue in Lloydtown.

Time travel at the Sharon Temple

Less than an hour's drive from Toronto, discover a unique bit of history amid the rapid sprawl in the town of Sharon.

The Temple of the Children of Peace

Properly undertaken, a visit to the 1825 Temple of the Children of Peace in the village of Sharon should be approached more as a pilgrimage than a mere excursion. This enigmatic monument of Christian mysticism, its every column and beam suffused with arcane symbolism, is not only the most sublimely proportional building ever erected in Upper Canada, it is the cradle of Canadian democracy: a holy place built to nurture the spirit of liberalism, co-operation and tolerance in a deeply reactionary, raw-boned colony. Other reasons to visit? Eight historic buildings, over one and a half hectares of parkland, heritage herb gardens and over 7,000 artifacts.

• Children of the Peace

Tory Toronto laughed at the Children of Peace when they trundled down Yonge Street in their ox wagon, all

The Sharon Temple, a national historic site.

dressed in white, to sing accompaniments to the biblical harangues of their leader, the charismatic David Willson, a former Quaker. But the Children had the last laugh: Under Willson's talented leadership, they transformed their successful co-operative community — which included a meeting house, temple, schools, general store, post office, cider and gristmill, blacksmith, tinsmith and shoemaker — into the heartland of democratic reform in Upper Canada.

 While you are here, why not visit a more recent artifact? The drive-in movie theatre! **Stardust Drive-In** at 893 Mount Albert Road in Newmarket has three digital screens, video games and a snack bar. Bring a lawn chair and watch the movie outside.

◆ Political Reform

It was here that the Reform Association, predecessor of the modern Liberal Party, first convened. Most famously, it was here that Willson and Reform leader Robert Baldwin arranged the local election of Quebec's Louis-Hippolyte LaFontaine, a historic gesture that marked the first time anybody had conceived of Canada as a single nation comprising French and English as equal partners.

Working together, and without a shot being fired, LaFontaine and Baldwin resisted violent opposition to break Canada's colonial shackles and create the country we know today. The Sharon Temple — coincidentally but fittingly — is the finest possible memorial of their peaceable vision.

Also fittingly, the temple inspired one of the earliest efforts at historical preservation in Canada. That, combined with the excellence of its con-

If the grounds of Temple Sharon whet your appetite for the outdoors, visit nearby **Rogers Reservoir Conservation Area**, where you can hike, cycle or watch for nesting birds. Parking is available off of Green Lane and Concession Road 2.

struction, means it has never needed actual restoration. In this country at least, the Sharon Temple is the ultimate expression of the word "original."

The farmhouse of Ebenezer Doan, master builder of the temple.

Other artifacts of the Children of Peace are arranged around the temple grounds, including Willson's equally elegant and eccentric study as well as the relocated farmhouse of the temple's master builder, Ebenezer Doan. The temple and grounds are open to visitors from Wednesday to Sunday between May and October.

The Cemetery

If you're susceptible to the spell of this place, you will probably want to visit the Sharon Burying Ground, located just south of the village, on the east side of busy Leslie Street. In use since 1820, this is where many of the original Children of Peace are buried, including both Willson and Doan and their families. It is a serene and moody counterpart to the incessant noise and activity of the encroaching suburbs.

The Sharon Burying Ground is both enchanting and slightly eerie.

Delight in the *Credit River Valley*

& CALEDON

The upper valley of the Credit River marks an important place in the geology of our region: It's where the Niagara Escarpment meets the Oak Ridges Moraine, and where the flat plain of Toronto gets most thoroughly rumpled and recreational opportunities are most concentrated.

Like so many of the valley lands that have grown into a kind of green girdle around the spreading city, these ones endured a rough introduction to bare-knuckle civilization. The Credit Valley is rife with monuments of the pioneer water-powered industries

that once existed here (including, I am proud to note, the ruins of the Barber Dynamo, the continent's first hydro-electric power plant, in the gorge south of Georgetown). But the quarries, mills and kilns that once carved up and despoiled the landscape are — for the most part — long gone, and rowdy labour camps like the aptly named Brimstone are now famous beauty spots.

Drive the Forks of the Credit Road

This is a driving destination, indeed a famous one. Anyone who has ever owned a sports car in Toronto likely knows the Forks of the Credit Road, which departs the grid west of Highway 10, about 15 kilometres north of Brampton, swoops down into the valley, snakes along the river and switchbacks up to the tableland 7 kilometres later. It's the best stretch of driving road anywhere near Toronto, and as such suffers from its share of city traffic. But it's always fun to drive — or ride, if you're not afraid of Camaros. The Forks will be your starting point for exploring the hikes and rest stops that follow.

The winding Forks of the Credit Road is spectacular during the fall.

Ascend Devil's Pulpit

The steepest trail in this hilly country is also its most rewarding: the 100-metre climb to the limestone outcrop known as Devil's Pulpit (from which the name for nearby Brimstone no doubt came). It begins at the intersection of Chisholm Street on the south side of the Forks of the Credit Road and climbs almost straight up to a famous view. A cable strung alongside the steepest section is a welcome aid.

Along the way, the relatively new Ring Kiln Side Trail detours along the face of the escarpment to the eerie ruins

of what was once a major industrial installation, where rock was burned into lime, now lost to triumphant nature.

Forks of the Credit Provincial Park

Forks of the Credit Provincial Park was one of the first fruits of Len Gertler's groundbreaking Niagara Escarpment study of 1968, and even today one look at the surrounding landscape — devastatingly enormous gravel pits — speaks to the urgency of that initiative. But the oasis-like park tucked in behind the pits includes the densest, least-travelled network of walking and cycling trails in the area. This is where the Bruce and Trans Canada Trails meet in a lumpy intersection. The park also includes a long stretch of undisturbed, publicly accessible fishing water along the Credit.

You can hike or cycle into the park along the Bruce Trail, which follows Dominion Street north from the Forks of the Credit Road through the now-sleepy hollow at Brimstone. But the greatest variety of trails is accessible from the park's main entrance on McLaren Road, which crosses the Forks of the Credit Road 3 kilometres west of Highway 10. The entrance is 3 kilometres north on McLaren.

Take a Break in Belfountain

At the top of the Forks of the Credit Road is the hamlet of Belfountain, with two busy cafés catering to excursionists. Here you can also stretch your legs with a quick descent back

Forks of the Credit Provincial Park.

The suspension bridge in Belfountain Conservation Area.

into the valley through the Belfountain Conservation Area, which owes much of its scenic topography — a bell-topped fountain, a waterfall, a cave and a bridge — to Edwardian-worthy Charles Mack, "inventor of the cushion-backed rubber stamp." Originally designed to grace his country estate, Mack's handiwork is now especially popular with wedding parties. There are two short but steep loop trails through the grounds, although you can continue down the steep Trimble Side Trail toward the Forks and the main Bruce Trail.

Enjoy Erin

Straddling the west fork of the Credit just upriver from Belfountain, the picturesque village of Erin somehow stays off the beaten track despite offering some of the area's best shopping and dining along its Main Street. Here you can also visit the Porcupine's Quill, an artisanal publisher that has become a CanLit legend for the quality and, especially, the beauty of its work over the past 40 years. If you wish to visit, be sure to book an appointment in advance by calling 519-833-9158.

Terra Cotta Conservation Area

This conservation area, south of the Forks and near the town of Terra Cotta, is a slightly more developed alternative to Forks of the Credit Provincial Park, although less so than it once was, with former parking lots now revegetated and a swimming pool replaced by a

wetland. Of the former campground, nine select picnic sites remain amid the park's 185 hectares, but there is still a pavilion with washrooms and a snack bar. Cross-country ski rentals and lessons are available in the winter, and 6 kilometres of the trails are groomed for skiing.

Terra Cotta Conservation Area.

CYCLING THE CALEDON HILLS

Every four corners wants to be a cycling mecca these days, but the **Caledon Hills** are the real thing, long a magnet for serious mountain and road cyclists. But be warned: considering the terrain of the escarpment, the moraine and the valley, the operative word here is "hills."

Members of the Caledon Cycling Club, one of the largest in Ontario, meet regularly at the **Caledon Hills Cycling** shop in the village of **Inglewood** for long and varied rides throughout the region. But you needn't be a member to take advantage of the inside knowledge: As well as providing all of the equipment and logistical support you might need, the shop, which is located at 15640 McLaughlin Road, publishes detailed maps for a prime selection of local rides on its website, caledonhillscycling.com.

Perhaps the most popular, family-friendly route in the region is the **Caledon Trailway**, which runs along a former railbed from **Terra Cotta** 35 kilometres east to **Palgrave**, passing through **Cheltenham**, **Caledon East** and Inglewood on the way. Caledon boasts that its rail trail is the first officially designated section of the Trans Canada Trail, and it commemorates the distinction with a pavilion in a park at the halfway point in the village of Caledon East. The trail now also forms part of the **Greenbelt Cycling Route**.

NORTH

Enjoy the Headwaters

The fact that such a place as "The Headwaters" now exists shows just how successful the recent re-naturalization of Toronto's hinterland has been. Like the watershed-based conservation districts that have led the change, it is a new kind of place defined by its nature — in this case, a high, rolling upland — rather than municipal borders. The name comes from four rivers — the Humber, Credit, Nottawasaga and Grand — all of which originate in the high country around Orangeville.

The Headwaters is the heart of horse country in Ontario.

The Headwaters, only 45 minutes from Toronto, makes a perfect day trip where you can enjoy the outdoors on foot, horseback or skis.

Horse Riding

With a population of 23,000 horses, the Headwaters is the heart of Ontario's equine country, with a concentration of stables, events, breeders and trainers dense enough to create its own economy. Most of the stables cater to serious riders, but many also offer trail rides to more casual day trippers and are sure to appeal to children.

• Rawhide Adventures, one of the best known of these ranches, offers a real variety of experiences, including trail rides and roundups, on a working cattle ranch northeast of Shelburne. Check rawhide-adventures.on.ca for bookings and directions.

• Little Creek Ranch, located just south of Highway 89 on the Mono-Adjala Townline, offers riding instruction and horsemanship, a family "afternoon with horses" (including refreshments) and an apiary. According to the Headwaters tourist bureau, Little Creek Ranch offers the area's "Best Agri-Tourism Experience." Contact Elaine Capes at ecapes2017@gmail.com or 705-716-4445 for more information.

• The Fallbrook Trail Ranch (formerly Wildwood Manor Ranch) is the closest of them all, located just the other side of Georgetown. It offers lessons as well as group and private trail rides. See fallbrooktrail.com for more information.

TOWNING AROUND

The area's well-preserved towns and villages are well worth a visit, too.

Cheltenham: A cozy town with many designated heritage properties, like the general store that overlooks the Credit River. The Spirit Tree Estate Cidery is a three-minute drive away.

Alton: A quiet, historic village that is home to the Alton Mill Arts Centre, which has studios, galleries, shops, a café and a museum.

Mono Centre: Visit Peter Cellar's Pub, the unique basement bar in Mono Cliffs Inn.

Shelburne: This farming community is home to two local traditions that will take you back in time: the Heritage Music Festival, including fiddling and barn-dancing, and the Shelburne Fall Fair.

Orangeville: It won't make the top of any tourist's to-do list, but a visit to downtown Orangeville can make for a pleasant side trip. Broadway is a handsome main street, well worth exploring, and the Orangeville Farmers' Market, held on Saturdays throughout the summer, has been leading the local food movement for almost 30 years.

- Finally, Teen Ranch, the busy Christian sports camp located just south of Orangeville, hosts private trail rides all year long. See teenranch.com for more information.

Skiing around the Headwaters
◆ Downhill

The Hockley Valley Resort is easy to get to, albeit tiny. To find it, turn west onto Hockley Road off Airport Road, 7 kilometres north of Highway 9.

Another 20 kilometres north on Airport Road will bring you to the slightly more impressive Mansfield Ski Club, which is unfortunately closed to non-members on weekends.

◆ Cross-Country

Mansfield Outdoor Centre, one of the most pleasant cross-country ski areas south of Barrie, has 40 kilometres of groomed trails and a rustic farmhouse chalet with equipment rentals and a snack bar. They also offer a 10-kilometre dedicated skate-skiing loop.

The Mono Nordic Ski Club, with 20 kilometres of groomed trails and a heated chalet, is even closer. You can find it west of Highway 10 on Monora Park Drive, 3 kilometres north of Orangeville.

Finally, there are the Hockleycrest Ski Trails, which run alongside the Bruce Trail on lands generously made available by five nearby landowners, including the Taoist Tai Chi Society and the Coptic Church. The trails are groomed but no other facilities are available. The entrance is located just east of Airport Road (Dufferin Road 18) on Adjala Sideroad 5, just 4 kilometres north of Highway 9.

ALL ABOARD! THE SOUTH SIMCOE STEAM HERITAGE RAILWAY

Thanks to the miracle of obsolete technology, the formerly arduous journey from **Tottenham** to **Beeton** can now be accomplished in the relative comfort of a century-old steam train. Kick back and enjoy a guided excursion on the historic **South Simcoe Railway** that begins in Tottenham, located 20 kilometres west of Highway 401 on Highway 9. It takes about an hour to complete the journey to Beeton and back. Fall colour excursions are especially popular and need to be booked well in advance. Read the schedule carefully to ensure your train will be pulled by the real thing — a steam locomotive — rather than a vintage diesel unit.

BRUCE TRAIL ADVENTURES NO. 1

Mono Cliffs Provincial Park

This is the closest and most popular destination for Toronto's hikers. It's a geologist's wonderland, with a varied network of well-marked side trails and loops branching off the main trunk of the Bruce Trail, which runs through the middle of the park. With its 30-metre cliffs and canyon trail, the park is home to a diversity of ferns and cedars.

To get there, follow Airport Road 12 kilometres north of Highway 9 and turn west onto Dufferin Road 8. After 4 kilometres, turn north again on the 3rd Line EHS. There is a pay-and-display parking lot and a good trail map at the park entrance. Alternatively, you can park in the village of Mono Centre and hike north from there.

Boyne Valley Provincial Park

A little farther north, Boyne Valley Provincial Park contains another, slightly less extensive network of loops on the main Bruce Trail. There are no maps or facilities here, but neither are there any parking or entrance fees. The park is located a few kilometres north of the hamlet of Primrose at the intersection of Highways 10 and 89. See brucetrail.org for information on routes and access.

NORTH

Tour the Minesing Wetlands & CREEMORE

For those with a taste for the unusual, Minesing Wetlands offers a hidden wilderness adventure astonishingly close to home. Stop by Creemore for a meal and a local beer afterward, or spend a whole day — its small-town main street is quieter and less touristy than the resort areas to the north.

The Minesing Wetlands

Many drivers who have attempted to dodge a traffic jam on the way home from cottage country have reason to curse the Minesing Wetlands, a large, intractable block of impassable terrain

A peaceful paddle through the Minesing Wetlands.

that combines with Lake Simcoe to make the bustling city of Barrie an almost perfect bottleneck. But to a savvy minority, this huge complex of fens, marshes and swamps is a magnet — the Okefenokee of the north, offering an outdoor experience that is all but unique in Ontario.

Exploring this watery realm, drained by the Nottawasaga River, makes for an easy day trip, but it is no straightforward downstream float. The challenge is navigation, especially during high water, when the swamps are most extensive and easy-to-follow river channels disappear. Canoeists get lost here all the time. Much of the equipment one would take on a wilderness trip — especially a map

and compass or GPS — is necessary for safety's sake. You will also need to arrange a shuttle to leave a car or bike at the take-out point, as loops are impossible here.

The Minesing Wetlands make for a captivating day trip outdoors.

HISTORIC FORT WILLOW

Once a vital depot in the War of 1812 but lost in the woods today, historic **Fort Willow** recalls the long-standing importance of Huronia at a time when the land was defined by rivers and portages rather than roads. There's not much to see inside its sharpened-stake stockade, but there are washroom facilities and hiking trails nearby. To find it, turn west off George Johnston Road onto Portage Road, located 2 kilometres south of the Willow Creek Canoe Corral.

For all those reasons, joining a guided trip is probably the best way to explore Minesing. They are offered by Friends of Minesing Wetlands (minesingwetlands.ca), the Barrie Canoe and Kayak Club and Eagle Adventures (eagleadventureexperiences.com).

Getting There

Although there are other access points, Willow Creek provides the most popular route into the wetlands. To get there, exit Highway 400 at Dunlop Street (Highway 90) in Barrie, travel west to George Johnston Road and north 8 kilometres to the Willow Creek Canoe Corral. The 19-kilometre canoe route follows Willow Creek to its confluence with the Nottawasaga River and then down to the Nottawasaga to the Edenvale Conservation Area on Highway 26. Alternatively, you can enter from the south, near the town of Angus, on either the Mad River or the Nottawasaga itself. All the wetland routes end at the Edenvale Conservation Area. The Nottawasaga Valley Conservation Authority (nvca.on.ca) publishes a useful and informative route map.

Creemore

There's always at least one good reason to visit the hamlet of Creemore, tucked into the shadow of the escarpment near the head of the Mad River. In a province now swimming in craft beer, Creemore Springs Brewery stands as a pioneer, remaining "proudly 100 years behind the times" since its creation in 1987. Success led to the company's acquisition by brewing giant Molson in 2005, which dented its status as a craft brewery, but the handful of beers produced here are still fire-brewed one batch at a time, using only four ingredients, including water that's trucked in daily from a nearby artesian well. Located in a former hardware store at 139 Mill Street, the brewery offers tours (with free samples of its products) daily from noon.

A stately looking home in the leafy village of Creemore.

But the village would reward a trip even without the beer, with its compact collection of surprisingly chic stores and restaurants catering to the weekend gentry scattered about the nearby hills. The Hundred Mile Store on Mill Street purveys locally grown organic food, while Curiosity House Books and Gallery is the focus of local literary life. Heirloom 142, also on Mill Street, sells sophisticated country decor.

Every July, the village is overrun by motor traffic, arriving in the form of hundreds of classic and vintage vehicles competing in the Creemore Valley Classics car show, one of the province's most popular regional car shows. Visit creemorevalleyclassics.com to learn more.

The exterior of Creemore Springs Brewery.

Getting There

To find Creemore from Minesing, follow County Road 10 west through the town of Angus, and turn west again (left) at County Road 9.

Discover Orillia

NORTH

ARTS & TARTS

This town at the Narrows between Lakes Simcoe and Couchiching could claim to be the oldest inhabited place in Ontario, due to an extraordinary artifact that first entered recorded history when the explorer Samuel de Champlain noted its existence in 1615. Portions of the Mnjikaning Fish Weirs — wooden stakes driven into the silt to help corral and net fish — are 5,000 years old, dating from a time when Stonehenge itself was no more than a circle of wooden posts.

Called "Tkaronto" in the Iroquoian language, this place was sufficiently important for its name to travel south to describe the route taken to get there from Lake Ontario. Hence the meaning of our own Toronto: sticks in the mud.

"GET YOUR BOOTS TO THE ROOTS"

This is the motto for the **Orillia Farmers' Market**. Dating back to 1842, it is one of the longest-running farmers' markets in the province. On top of the great farm-raised meat, fresh-picked produce and prepared foods, it's an enjoyable place to have a coffee and listen to local musicians. It is open Saturdays year-round at the **Orillia Public Library**, which is located at the corner of Mississaga Street and West Street.

A summer street festival in Orillia.

Mostly submerged now and overshadowed by the bridge that carries Highway 12 over the Narrows, the weirs offer little to the eye. There is a plaque marking them at the end of Bridge Street, on the eastern side of the narrows, and an ambitious plan is afoot to create a new pedestrian bridge and interpretation centre at the site.

The town itself is doing its utmost to recover its 19th-century status as a touristic hot spot, using art as the impetus. Local resident and indefatigable Orillia booster Charles Pachter is leading the effort to turn the town into a major destination on the international arts trail. But for many people, the most compelling reason to visit Orillia is to savour its signature cultural achievement — its cuisine.

Classic Canadian Butter Tarts

The simple, homegrown butter tart is said to be one of the few delicacies of purely Canadian origin, and in central Ontario it has become a fetish. There are as many butter tart competitions as there are fall fairs. There is a Butter Tart Trail in Wellington City and a Butter Tart Tour in the Kawarthas. Media

Butter tarts from Wilkies Bakery may be the most delectable reason to visit Orillia.

point for a tour of what Pachter calls Orillia's increasingly "funky and fun" downtown.

The Arts Scene Comes Alive!

The focal point of the town's cultural ambition today is the Orillia Museum of Art and History at 30 Peter Street South, just off Mississaga, which has grown into a vital institution with an ambitious exhibition schedule. One highlight is the annual Carmichael Canadian Landscape Exhibition in the fall, named in honour of Orillia native and Group of Seven member Franklin Carmichael. This and other exhibitions explore local heritage in a much more

revel in the burning question of who makes the best butter tarts, and new contenders appear by the dozen every year. It's all a bit much.

But there is an answer: No other bakery has won more consistent plaudits for the quality of its tarts than Wilkies at 169 Mississaga Street East. For many, it is a place of pilgrimage. It's also an excellent starting

PUBLIC ART: CHAMPLAIN MONUMENT

Nearby **Couchiching Beach Park** is dominated by a far grander piece of public art, once the town's glory and now something of an embarrassment: the towering bravura **Samuel de Champlain Monument**, created by British sculptor Vernon March and installed in 1924 to celebrate white supremacy, Canadian style. It's a brilliant work that both misrepresents Champlain as a conquering hero and reduces his Indigenous allies to overawed supplicants. Cleverly, the town is now co-operating with the Chippewas of Rama First Nation to create a corrective piece for installation nearby. It will make for an interesting dialogue.

sophisticated way than one is likely to encounter in a small-town museum.

Located under the town's landmark clock tower, the Orillia Museum of Art and History has helped spawn an emerging scene known as the Peter Street Arts District, comprising half a dozen galleries and related businesses. The district comes to life every summer with the kickoff of Streets Alive!, a summer-long exhibit that adorns the town with dozens of inventive variations on a common artifact: doors one year, guitars another, chairs the next.

Summer culminates in late August with the Orillia Starry Night Studio and Gallery Tour. There are an impressive 35 stops on this annual walking tour, including Pachter's MOFO Moose Factory of Orillia.

Opening night of an exhibition at the Orillia Museum of Art and History.

LEFT
Street art projects bring local artists' works to life in downtown Orillia.

The boathouse at the Stephen Leacock Museum.

Leacock Museum National Historic Site

Despite its contemporary ambitions, Orillia is still best known to Canadians as the model for Mariposa, the bumptious backwater immortalized by Stephen Leacock in his comic masterpiece *Sunshine Sketches of a Little Town*. Honouring the association, Orillia maintains the author's elegant summer home as the Leacock Museum National Historic Site. It's a drafty, low-slung manor that convincingly evokes a golden era of genteel cottaging, with croquet and hooped skirts on an ample lawn that Leacock called "the frontier of the sunshine."

Carefully restored and furnished with artifacts of the author's life and work, the museum also houses art exhibitions and events. It is located on Old Brewery Bay, just east of the Narrows. To find it, take Forest Avenue north of Atherley Road and turn east onto Museum Drive.

Mariposa Folk Festival

Orillia's fictional identity also lives on in the form of the Mariposa Folk Festival, held annually over three days in early July. It is the longest running festival of its kind in Canada. Having moved from its 1961 birth in Orillia to Toronto and back, the festival now

makes its home in Tudhope Park on the shore of Lake Couchiching. The park has a lovely beach and a somewhat less lovely bronze statue of Orillia's other famous son, singer Gordon Lightfoot.

What makes this festival stand out from the crowd of summer music festivals, apart from its pedigree and its stellar lineup of Canadian and international acts, is its family-friendly atmosphere, including a children's stage. Mariposa is a mash-up of music and dance acts, performance workshops, spoken word, food trucks and artisans. There's camping on site, so you can come for the day or the weekend.

Bruce Cockburn performs at the 2017 Mariposa Folk Festival.

CASINO RAMA

For most visitors to the region, Orillia is just the last traffic snarl to be endured before ascension to the gambler's heaven of **Casino Rama**, the largest First Nations casino in Canada, located at 5899 Rama Road. With 10 restaurants and a 5,000-seat theatre hosting top-name entertainment, it's a world unto itself. Whatever one thinks of the action there, it is interesting to note that the Indigenous Peoples once pushed from the favoured Narrows into the comparatively barren Rama Township to make room for Orillia are now the town's leading employers.

See Sainte-Marie among the Hurons,

WYE MARSH & DISCOVERY HARBOUR

An appealing trifecta of genuine attractions waits at the end of the drive to Midland and Penetanguishene on the southernmost shores of Georgian Bay: Sainte-Marie among the Hurons, Wye Marsh and Discovery Harbour. All three owe their existence to initiatives of the federal government, which makes them unique in these pages and, in the case of the mission at Sainte-Marie, uniquely important. All three are amazing interpretive experiences for kids and adults alike.

Sainte-Marie among the Hurons

Every nation originates in an epic, and there is no place better suited to imagine and understand the epic of Canada than here. Not at Quebec, the capital of New France, but here in the *pays d'en haut*, where the bright promise of a genuine European-Indigenous alliance met and tragically failed its first stern test.

The basic shape of the tale follows a well-known, sad pattern of cultural collision, disease and warfare, as repeated throughout the continent in the first

centuries post-contact. The story of the Jesuit mission to the Wendat (formerly Huron) people stands apart in its extremes: both in the earnest good intentions of the Europeans and the magnitude of their comeuppance.

The result was two martyred saints of the Catholic Church and the destruction of an entire nation. Following the conquest of Sainte-Marie and Huronia by the Haudenosaunee (also known as the Iroquois) in 1648, southern Ontario remained a no man's land for decades.

This is no ordinary pioneer village. Thanks to the Jesuits' conscientious record-keeping in their *Relations*, the tragedy of Sainte-Marie is a recurring fixture of our literature. Among modern retellings, both Brian Moore's *Black Robe* and Joseph Boyden's *The Orenda* stand out as exceptional. Reading either would be excellent preparation for a visit. Bruce Beresford's 1991 film of the Moore novel also stands up well.

Every one of the 30-odd buildings, filled with artifacts, clustered behind the pointed-stick stockade that surrounds Sainte-Marie today is new, having been painstakingly rebuilt from archaeological findings and documentary sources. But the spell of the past

A view of the European compound at Sainte-Marie among the Hurons.

Visitor can see birds of prey up close at Wye Marsh on Sundays.

ABOVE
The exterior of one of the Wendat longhouses.

is genuine, and nowhere more so than in the details: the narrow beds where the Europeans slept; the crude, dimly lit desk where the priests composed their *Relations*; the peltries hanging in the First Nations longhouses, a lacrosse stick leaning against a bunk.

The two longhouses — one for Christian Wendat and a second, literally beyond the pale, for non-believers — are especially impressive. An adjoining museum makes for a worthwhile linger.

To get to Sainte-Marie from Toronto, follow Highway 400 north to Highway 93. Drive north on Highway 93 then east on Highway 12 for 5 kilometres. Sainte-Marie is open from the beginning of May until Thanksgiving. See saintemarieamongthehurons.on.ca for detailed information and events.

Wye Marsh Wildlife Centre

Right next door to the mission, the quiet stream that carried the last Wendat refugees to safety is now home to the Wye Marsh Wildlife Centre. Novel when it first opened in 1969, the centre has served as a model for subsequent efforts to promote conservation by connecting modern city dwellers with nature. It's a compact operation that's dense with diversions, including hiking and ski trails, canoe rentals for paddling the marsh and — the main event — plenty of wildlife to observe up close.

There's a bevy of swans that patrol the marsh year-round, but the big

draw here is always the centre's large collection of captive birds of prey. You can visit them in their cages any time or, for the best experience, show up on Sundays at 1 p.m. for the centre's "live" birds of prey show.

Snakes and turtles populate the Interpretive Centre, home to educational displays about wetlands and their inhabitants.

Discovery Harbour

Discovery Harbour commemorates what was once His Majesty's Naval Establishment on Lake Huron, an important military outpost built after the War of 1812 in anticipation of renewed invasion from the United States. For decades after, the harbour and its camp were the British military's sole presence in Canada. This Lake Huron harbour is far away from "the briny ocean tossed," but it's entirely authentic and unique in Ontario.

◆ Ships of State

Two replica 19th-century schooners line the wharf, with gangplanks and costumed sailors to welcome visitors aboard. The largest faithfully recreates the warship H.M.S. *Tecumseth*, named for the Shawnee leader who had died fighting alongside the British a year before the ship's commission in 1814.

Wye Marsh Wildlife Centre.

You'll find **Awenda Provincial Park** a short drive away from Discovery Harbour. Pack a picnic lunch and enjoy the park's beautiful beaches.

The recreated H.M.S. *Tecumseth* at Discovery Harbour.

The original H.M.S. *Tecumseth* sank at its mooring in the long peace that followed, but it was pulled from the harbour in the mid-1950s. Only recently has the wreck received its proper due, now lying in dignified repose, like the remains of a Viking ship, at the H.M.S. *Tecumseth* Centre.

Onshore buildings at Discovery Harbour recreate the life of the once-isolated military outpost, where only the stone-built Officers Quarters survived intact. They include the Naval Surveyors House, where the pioneer mapmaker Henry Bayfield planned and carried out his famous surveys of the upper lakes, charting no fewer than 20,000 islands in Lake Huron alone.

Located at 93 Jury Drive in Penetanguishene, Discovery Harbour is open seven days a week between Victoria Day and Labour Day. There is a licensed restaurant on site.

WATERFRONT EATING

Both Penetanguishene and Midland have attractive waterfronts where you can enjoy a lovely view with your lunch. The **Boathouse Eatery** has a patio on the Midland Town Dock, while Penetanguishene Harbour hosts the **World Famous Dock Lunch**, a local landmark since 1957. In nearby Victoria Harbour, east of Sainte-Marie on Highway 12, you will find the **Queen's Quay British Pub and Restaurant**.

NORTH

Splash around Wasaga Beach

Toronto's long-time favourite summer beach resort presents an interesting inversion of the typical tourist-trap phenomenon, in which tacky development threatens to overwhelm the place's natural attraction. Here, fortunately, the famous beach is in fine shape — super clean, safe and carefully managed as part of Wasaga Beach Provincial Park (a day-use park). The sunsets are incredible, too.

The problem is the tacky, which has declined steadily since its postwar heyday and hit bottom when a fire destroyed most of Wasaga's beachfront businesses in 2007. Various redevelopment schemes have come and gone. So there it rests, bereft and forlorn where it was once lively, fun and truly tacky.

BONUS BEACHES

If Wasaga seems too hectic and crowded on a summer weekend, a short drive north on Tiny Beaches Road will bring you to a long series of smaller strands with a more local appeal. **Balm Beach** is a perfectly quaint example of an old-fashioned public resort. Farther north again, **Awenda Provincial Park** has five public beaches on Georgian Bay, and the fabled **Giants Tomb Island** is just offshore to the north.

Wasaga is the first Ontario provincial park to earn "Blue Flag" status for the cleanliness and environmental integrity of its beaches. The park has come a long way from the days when folks used to race stock cars along the strand.

And, yes, you can still play minigolf, slurp ice cream and buy cheap souvenirs at Wasaga Beach. The town programs events throughout the summer and stages free concerts.

Sun, Sand and Swim

Wasaga Beach has six official subdivisions, numbered from east to west. Beach Areas 1 and 2 are at the centre of the action, and the remaining beaches stretch 10 kilometres to the west, getting progressively less crowded. Each has its own parking lot. The wide

An aerial view of Wasaga Beach, which hugs the sparkling waters of Georgian Bay.

The summer crowds, however, disguise the lingering barrenness, and they are still reliable: It is said that two million tourists a year enjoy this place, attracted by the longest freshwater beach in the world, superior to anything found on the lower lakes. Clear Georgian Bay water is a huge draw, and

REVVED-UP RECREATION

One of the newest and most popular events is the **Wasaga Beach Motorcycle Rally,** an annual event held over a July weekend that attracts hundreds of bikers to the beach and nearby roads. There are prizes for the loudest exhaust pipes as well as two concert stages featuring a world-class collection of classic rock tribute bands.

A little bit out of town, **Wasaga Beach Paintball** (wasagapaintball.com) claims to be "Canada's premier paintball and laser combat megapark." It has been spreading the splatter since 1992. **Skydive Wasaga Beach** (skydivewasagabeach.com) is a more recent entry offering an even more thrilling (and expensive) service.

And what would a beach resort be without minigolf? **Skull Island Mini Putt** (skullisland.ca) is an 18-hole course that takes you to a lost island in the Caribbean, complete with waterfalls, swaying palms and scurvy-dog pirates. The course is open May to Labour Day.

sandy beaches are perfect for relaxing and playing after a dip in the warm water. The play structures and shallow waters near Beach Area 5 make it the obvious choice for families with young kids. Beach Area 3 has an off-leash area for dogs. Kiteboarding, biking, birding and boating are also popular at the park (Beach Area 1 has a boat launch).

Nancy Island Historic Site and Welcome Centre

The bicentennial of the War of 1812 failed to arouse much attention elsewhere in the country, but Wasaga benefited from the gift of a new welcome centre, the Nancy Island Historic Site, located at 119 Mosley Street. Like the H.M.S. *Tecumseth* at Discovery Harbour (see pages 49–50), the Nancy was a topsail schooner that led an

eventful career during the war before being sunk by American forces while it hid at the mouth of the Nottawasaga River. An island of the same name formed around the wreck, which was recovered in the 1920s. It's now the centrepiece of an interesting small museum that provides unlikely respite in the centre of a busy beach town.

Festivals and events, like Kite Fest, draw visitors to Wasaga's beautiful beaches.

After a hot day in the sun at Wasaga Beach, visit **Grandma's Beach Treats** at 1014 Mosley Street (near 22nd Street) for ice cream — big portions and lots of flavours. Other treats at this friendly year-round shop include popcorn, brownies and butter tarts.

A piping plover chick.

RIGHT
A wintry scene in Wasaga Beach.

Ploverpalooza: Celebrating the Endangered Piping Plover

No sign of changing times is more telling than the latest festival to take hold of Wasaga Beach: Ploverpalooza. The event celebrates the return of the endangered piping plover to its historical nesting grounds on Wasaga Beach. Formerly wiped out in Ontario, this little shorebird has chosen a large protected area adjacent to the most popular beach in the province to stage its comeback. Wasaga-born chicks are now colonizing several other sites in the province, according to naturalists. Apart from protecting nesting birds, the main activity of the summer-long "festival" involves volunteers offering information about the birds and the occasional peek through a scope.

Winter Workout at the Wasaga Nordic Centre

An abundance of lake-effect snow makes Wasaga a reliable destination for cross-country skiing and snowshoeing, and the park is one of the few in the provincial system that caters to the sport, with 30 kilometres of groomed trails for skiers and another dozen for snowshoers. The longer trails rise up the forested dunes behind the flat shoreline, and there are warm-up huts in the interior. The Wasaga Nordic Centre is open for equipment rentals, snacks and warmth during the season. You can find it at 101 Blueberry Trail, across the river and south from Nancy Island.

The **Wasaga Nordic Centre** is also the starting points for over 50 kilometres of hiking trails, including the **Pine Trail** and sections of the **Ganaraska Trail**.

Get outdoors in Collingwood

& BLUE MOUNTAIN VILLAGE

A historic ship-building centre that transitioned easily into its post-industrial role as a recreational hot spot, Collingwood is located on Nottawasaga Bay in the southernmost part of Georgian Bay, just west of Wasaga Beach. It's best known as the gateway to the Blue Mountain Village and Resort, which has grown from a modest ski hill into an all-season magnet for outdoor fun. The town is also at the centre of some of the highest and most scenic sections and side trails of the popular Bruce Trail.

CROSS-COUNTRY SKIING

Downhill not your thing? Extensive escarpment skiing can be found south of Collingwood at **Highlands Nordic** cross-country ski resort near the village of Duntroon. This popular spot for keen cross-country skiers also offers 7 kilometres of snowshoe trails and a groomed toboggan hill. From Collingwood, drive south on Hurontario Street (Grey Road 124) to Duntroon, turn west on Grey Road 91 and watch for the sign atop the hill.

Winter at Blue Mountain Village.

The Blue Mountain Village

It's sad to think that these are the highest ski hills in southern Ontario, but a lot of Torontonians have had a lot of fun in the Blue so-called Mountains over the years. And we are an enterprising people, so much so that 75 years of steady development has transformed what was once a slanted apple orchard into the third-largest ski resort in Canada. Blue Mountain

Resort is also a leader in the development of all-season attractions, and it now offers an almost crazy variety of family activities year-round.

You can ride down the mountain on a rented bike or the Ridge Runner Mountain Coaster, zoom with friends on the Wind Rider Triple Zips, freefall 6.5 metres into the Apex Bag Jump, scramble the Woodlot Low Ropes or the Timber Challenge High Ropes, take an e-bike tour on local roads or even an off-road Segway tour. All in addition to the usual golf courses, tennis courts, swimming pools, restaurants and lodging. The creation of a pedestrian village at the base of the hill added shopping to the attractions at Blue.

Wondering where to eat? Blue Mountain Village has just about anything you want from snacks to fancy fare, breakfast, burgers and more. Try **Sunset Grill, Copper Blues** or **Firehall Pizza Co.**

The prices for individual activities are not ridiculous, but your plastic will be warm from swiping at the end of the day. The advantage is that every experience is well organized and accessible. Both the resort and other local outfitters also conduct guided tours of nearby, off-resort attractions, including some of the most scenic day hikes in the province.

As for downhill skiing — oh, that — Blue Mountain is still the highest publicly accessible hill this side of the Laurentians. Fast lifts, advanced snow-making and big-league efficiency compensate for its lack of vertical stature.

Blue Mountain has lots to offer beyond winter skiing.

ORGANIZED TOURS

Collingwood is an ideal destination for day trippers who prefer to leave the logistics to others. Blue Mountain Resort itself offers a number of off-site activities, including free guided hikes every day throughout the summer. **Eagle Adventures** (eagleadventureexperiences.com) offers a wide array of nature-themed day tours such as kayaking, canoeing, caving and rock climbing, as does **Free Spirit Tours** (freespirit-tours.com). **OSM Adventure Travel** (osmadventuretravel.com) specializes in boat tours and fishing. **Collingwood Cycling Tours** (collingwoodcyclingtours.com) serves two-wheelers, while **Xtreme Adventures** (xtremeadventures.ca) offers motorized sport in the form of jet skis and four-by-four Hummers.

The Scenic Caves Nature Adventures

Located just south of Blue Mountain Village, the Scenic Caves is a long-standing local attraction that has retained its small-scale character despite the impressively international clientele it now attracts. For summer activities, treetop walking, zip-lining and minigolf have joined the classic cave walk. In winter, the facility becomes the only full-service cross-country ski centre in Collingwood, with a compact and gentle trail network perfect for children and beginners. Summer or winter, don't miss the chance to cross the iconic 128-metre suspension bridge 25 metres above the valley floor. To find the scenic caves, follow Scenic Caves Road south from the village and up the mountain.

Scandinave Spa

Being in the bigs means that Blue Mountain has managed to attract such neighbours as Scandinave, an award-winning Scandinavian-style spa on its own 10 hectares just east of the village on Grey Road 21. It's beautiful, posh and sufficiently popular that casual visits for a sauna can often begin with a long chill on the wait-list. If you want a massage as well, prepare to book weeks in advance.

ABOVE Treetop trekking at the Scenic Caves.

After all the outdoor adventures are over, visitors can relax at the Scandinave Spa.

BRUCE TRAIL ADVENTURES NO. 2

The Collingwood area contains the highest elevations and some of the longest views of the entire Bruce Trail.

The Pretty River Loop

If you ask a local about their favourite hikes, they will almost certainly mention the Pretty River Loop. Advertising knows no higher truth than the name of this stream, which cuts an oversized valley through the escarpment just south of Collingwood and affords the finest views and hikes in the region. The trail is a classic Bruce Trail circuit, with as much elevation and scenery as any 5 kilometres in Ontario.

Len Gertler Side Trail

This trail through the **Loree Forest** is another especially scenic route that crosses the ridge of the Blue Mountains just above the private ski clubs that dominate their north-facing slopes. It combines with the main Bruce Trail to make another loop of about 5 kilometres. The side trail and the forest it traverses are named for the planner whose landmark *Niagara Escarpment Study*, published in 1968, first argued for the preservation of Ontario's most characteristic landform. Thanks to Len Gertler and the governments who took his advice, the escarpment has since been designated a UNESCO Biosphere Reserve.

Explore the Kolapore Uplands

& RAVENNA

For those who want backcountry skiing and snowshoeing rather than the familiarity of groomed trails, Kolapore, near Thornbury, offers some challenging trails. Stop by nearby Ravenna, which also offers hiking, climbing and wine tasting in the more temperate months.

Skiing the Kolapore Trails

No, this ain't B.C. You can't wake up in the morning and decide to spend the day traversing alpine meadows or skiing off peaks, but not all of the backcountry is 300 kilometres north of town. Closer even than Collingwood, the Kolapore Uplands are a vest-pocket wilderness with a 50-kilometre trail system maintained for the exclusive use of skiers who want to make their own tracks. Not for beginners, these trails are narrow, un-groomed and often steep. Facilities are non-existent, and dogs and snowshoes are not allowed. It's a serious skier's paradise.

The Kolapore trails are also maintained for hiking and mountain biking in the summer, where permitted by landowners and as volunteer resources permit.

Cross-country skiers enjoy the challenging trails in Kolapore.

The first thing you'll need before enjoying these trails is a map, and the best way to get one is from the Kolapore Wilderness Trails Association, the Collingwood-based group that maintains the system. To order one, visit kolaporetrails.org. (You can also join the group for a modest fee to support its efforts.) You'll need to carry extra clothes, water, food, a flashlight and a charged-up cell phone before starting out on these trails.

Getting There

The Kolapore trails are located just southwest of Collingwood. To reach them from Toronto, travel Highway 400 north to Barrie, go west on Highway 26 through Stayner and continue on County Roads 91 and 31 to Grey Road 2. There is a parking lot next to the trailhead on the east side of Grey Road 2, 6.5 kilometres to the north. See the Kolapore Wilderness Trails Association map for other access points.

RAVENNA COUNTRY MARKET
Your home base for your trips to Kolapore and Ravenna should be the **Ravenna Country Market** at 495572 Grey Road 2. This is where you will find the best local trip advice and fuel for your body: healthy, delicious homemade meals and snacks, to take out or eat in, with options for vegetarians. While you are re-energizing, browse the general store for local jam, honey and maple syrup, or relax outside — there are plenty of places to sit and enjoy the view.

Ravenna

A short drive from Kolapore, at the crossroads of Highway 2 and Grey Road 119, sits the tiny hamlet of Ravenna. In addition to its great general store, the Ravenna Country Market, it's also a hub for hiking, rock climbing, caving, cycling, apple picking and wine tasting.

• Metcalfe Rock

If you have no time for longer hikes in the Blue Mountains, you should consider a quick scramble up Metcalfe Rock, which yields a spectacular view west over Kolapore Creek Valley, especially in the fall. This is also a magnet for rock climbers, and several local outfitters offer tours and instruction. For more information, go to visitgrey.ca/business/metcalfe-rock.

• Georgian Hills Vineyards

If they can have vineyards on the north shore of Lake Ontario, why not the south shore of Georgian Bay? Georgian Hills Vineyards is pioneering the potential trend on the hills overlooking the bay. The wines are available at popular restaurants throughout the region, or you can visit the winery at 496350 Grey Road 2 for tastings paired with local artisanal cheeses and charcuterie. The tasting room is open year-round. Guided tours are also available. Visit georgianhillsvineyards.ca for more information.

ABOVE Ravenna Country Market is a great home base for exploring the area.

Outfitters offer winter tours of Metcalfe Rock.

• The Apple Pie Trail and TK Ferri Orchards

Let others chase butter tarts: It's all about apples in the Blue Mountains, a specialty showcased in the newly established Apple Pie Trail, which links dozens of culinary destinations — apple-related and otherwise — throughout the region. The Beaver Valley is home to many, including the Blackbird Pie Company in Heathcote and the Beaver Valley Orchard & Cidery in Kimberley. The newly open-to-the-public Thornbury Village Cider House at the river's mouth serves whole flights of alcoholic cider along with craft beers. See applepietrail.com for more details.

In season, you can pick your own apples at TK Ferri Orchards, located at 496415 Grey Road 2 (tkferriorchards.com). Their varieties include Honey Crisp, Mac, Ambrosia, Mutsu, Golden Delicious, Cortland and Gala. Pre-picked apples are also available at the market year-round.

The Beaver Valley Orchard & Cidery has a tasting room and offers free cidery tours.

LEFT
Apples are ripe for the picking in the fall at TK Ferri Orchards.

Visit Flesherton

& BEAVER VALLEY

The tiny, picturesque village of Flesherton is an ideal base for exploring Beaver Valley, free of the commercial vibe and crowds of nearby Collingwood.

Flesherton

Located at the juncture of Highway 10 and Grey Road 4, Flesherton is a hub for arts, culture and food. The Bicycle Café, at 14 Sydenham Street, is a local favourite for all-day cuisine and comfort food. Check out their Facebook page for live music events.

The Bicycle Café is a great spot to grab a fresh lunch or listen to some music.

The Flying Spatula Diner, at 125 Collingwood Street, is another great place to eat — enjoy a delicious all-day breakfast, a fresh to-go sandwich or a warm sit-down meal.

On Saturday mornings from May to Thanksgiving, visit the Flesherton and District Farmers' Market for fresh seasonal fruits and vegetables, premium meats, delicious baked goods, prepared foods and artisanal crafts.

The Flesherton Art Gallery showcases the arts and crafts of many of the artists who have long thrived in these tucked-away hills.

Cross-Country Skiing with the Glenelg Nordic Ski Club

If you'd prefer not to challenge the trails in Kolapore (see pages 60–61), Glenelg, near Flesherton, offers much the same experience but on groomed trails over tamer terrain. Like Kolapore, Glenelg is operated by volunteers and skied by members, but non-members are welcome. There is a drop box in the parking lot for trail fees. See glenelgnordicskiclub.org for more information.

To get to Glenelg, follow Highways 410 and 10 north through Brampton and Shelburne to Flesherton. In Flesherton, turn west (left) onto Grey Road 4 and then immediately north onto West Back Line. Travel 9.4 kilometres north and turn west onto Hamilton Lane. You'll find the Glenelg Nordic Ski Club parking lot 3.4 kilometres later at the intersection of Concession Road 8.

The enchanting trails of Glenelg.

BRUCE TRAIL ADVENTURES NO. 3
Beaver Valley

The wide, U-shaped valley of the **Beaver River** is a well-known beauty spot, wide open for exploration. You can take it all in from the top of **Old Baldy,** a limestone outcrop that rises more than 150 metres above the valley floor. In addition to the main Bruce Trail and its characteristic white blazes, the **Old Baldy Conservation Area** also includes side trails and loops maintained by the Grey Sauble Conservation Authority. This is one you can walk without an official trail guide. See greysauble.on.ca for more information and directions.

Hogg's Falls on the Boyne River is another prime hiking location in the upper valley, with easy access from the Lower Valley Road. For a more ambitious hike, you can follow the trail between here and **Eugenia Falls** on the Beaver, which is still impressive despite having been largely diverted for hydro power more than a century ago.

The Simcoe Snowbelt

Georgian Bay is a wonderful asset in Ontario, and one of its services is to create an old-fashioned, deep-snow winter all along its lee shore, beginning just an hour's drive north of the grim and greasy slush Torontonians call home during the winter months. It is rare even in the worst years not to find snow here, along with plenty of resorts serving those who seek it out. It's no Whistler, but the Simcoe Snowbelt is a reliable destination for easy family fun in what can be a difficult season.

Mount St. Louis Moonstone

Thanks to an epic bulldozer operation that added 15 crucial metres to its stature in the 1970s, Mount St. Louis Moonstone claims pre-eminence among local ski and snowboard resorts. It is certainly the most developed, with a dozen lifts capable of carrying an astonishing 23,600 people per hour — four times the throughput of the Sheppard subway line — up to its modest summit. So even on the busiest days (any winter weekend), it is always possible to spend more time on

MOUNT ST. LOUIS MOONSTONE

HARDWOOD SKI AND BIKE

the hill than waiting in line. "Louey" also negates its vertical challenge with terrain parks for snowboarders and freestyle skiers that are second to none in the province. See mountstlouis.com.

Horseshoe Valley Resort

Horseshoe Valley Resort can't match the numbers of its cross-valley rival, but it's more intimate and often less hectic. What sets it apart is an extensive cross-country operation, with 45 kilometres of well-groomed trails, including a long expert loop that will challenge the fittest skiers. The cross-country lodge is well equipped with gear for rent or sale, as well as an upstairs cafeteria with a warm fireplace nook. Curiously, the lingua franca in this chalet is Russian. See horseshoeresort.com.

Hardwood Ski and Bike

Hardwood Ski and Bike is the leading cross-country ski area in the Simcoe Snowbelt, perhaps in the province: it's the place where the most sanctioned races are held and the keenest skiers come to enjoy the most challenging trails. But there are also easy and intermediate trails for families and duffers to try. With the most youth programs and best cross-country instruction in the region, Hardwood is an ideal place to sample the sport. See hardwoodskiandbike.ca.

THE COPELAND FOREST

The Copeland Forest

Set between Mount St. Louis and Horseshoe Valley — and sprawling over more than 1,600 hectares — the Copeland Forest is "one of the loveliest forests in southern Ontario," according to the Ontario Trails Council. "It is super in spring, fabulous in fall."

Thanks to the work of the recently formed Copeland Forest Friends, it is also becoming an ideal place for winter enthusiasts to sample snowshoeing, winter hiking and back-country skiing without venturing far or making expedition-style preparations. The trails are shared by hikers, skiers, dog walkers and horseback riders, but if you venture off the trails you'll find there is a unique pleasure to gliding or trekking silently through the winter woods on untracked snow, particularly after a recent snowfall.

You can download a trail map at copelandfriends.ca or pick up a hard copy at the Esso station in the nearby hamlet of Craighurst.

To get to the Copeland Forest, exit Highway 400 onto Highway 93 East and make an immediate left onto Ingram Road, which traces the northwest edge of the forest. There is a plowed parking lot where "P2" is marked on the trail map. The parking lot is located on the south side of Ingram Road just past the intersection of Line 4. This is the best access point for un-groomed trails suitable for multi-use.

SOUTH

Exploring the country south of the lake reminds you of how fine-grained southern Ontario can be. It's right next door, it looks the same, but everything is slightly different: the climate, the vegetation, the crops, the geography, the history — even the accents. The sum of the differences is distinctiveness: No Torontonian has ever strolled north along Hamilton's James Street *toward* the lake without feeling it. And Hamilton, who knew? This long-scorned city now has lessons for its over-polished neighbour, including a gallery district unlike anything found in Toronto today. The first three entries of this chapter are devoted to this emerging slice of Ontario, one that merits multiple day trips for its diverse attractions.

For much of the world, Toronto itself is nothing more than a gateway to Niagara Falls, which attracts more tourists than all other tourist magnets in Ontario combined. But that's no reason to avoid it. The beaten path has its qualities, including decent public transit, a well-developed cycling infrastructure, a good selection of competitively priced package tours and a density of attractions you won't find anywhere else in Ontario — including the wineries that now rival the falls in their appeal.

There is certainly no more historic corner of the province. When people in Niagara talk about "the war," they're referring to one that ended 200 years ago. The War of 1812 remains a living presence in Niagara. Its monuments and battlefields create a deep impression that not even a fourth glass of Chardonnay can impair. Add the honky-tonk of Clifton Hill in Niagara Falls and, admittedly, the picture will get fuzzy. But on the whole it's gratifying that the setting of Ontario's most popular tourist attraction says so much about Canada and shows it off so well.

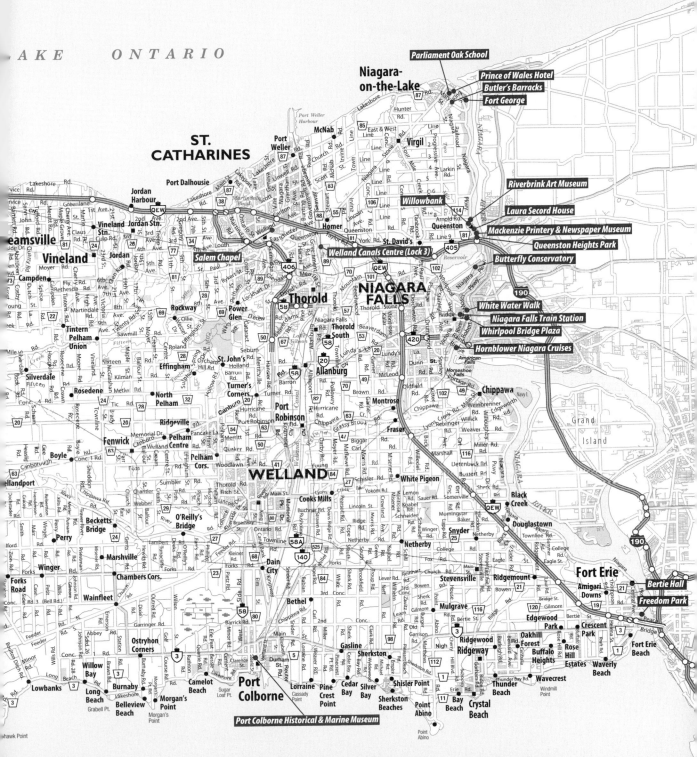

Discover *Hamilton*

ART & ARCHITECTURE

You can see all of Hamilton at a glance from the top of the Burlington Skyway, the view famously dominated by a long black wall of smoking, sometimes flaming steel mills. But the centre of interest today is what lies beyond. Like a fine old building scrubbed clean to reveal its original grandeur, Hamilton has emerged as a 21st-century model of recovering urbanism, full of character and interest. Seeing beyond the smokestacks not only reveals one of the oldest cities in Ontario, but also the greenest, comfortably enclosed in a dramatic natural landscape.

"Art Is the New Steel"

After decades of decay augmented by massively misbegotten attempts at urban renewal, downtown Hamilton is quickly, miraculously gentrifying — and the artists making it all happen are now firmly established as the fresh

The **McMaster Museum of Arts** is one of Canada's leading university art collections. It is located on the McMaster University campus, a short walk from the neighbourhood of Westdale Village. Admission is free.

faces of a new city. But the complex of galleries, studios and events they have created is no pale imitation of what big brother is doing eastward along the lake, where long-running gentrification has systematically extinguished a whole series of short-lived gallery districts. While it lasts, the contemporary arts scene in downtown Hamilton is unique.

Art Gallery of Hamilton

Nothing comes from nothing, and the Art Gallery of Hamilton (AGH), on King Street West, remains the fountain-head of this city's cultural life, having risen, fallen and risen again with the city itself. Although the AGH is now thoroughly modern and clothed in a stylish renovation by Hamilton-born architect Bruce Kuwabara, the heart of its appeal is a collection of 20th-century Canadian art that came together under the guidance of visionary curator T.R. MacDonald during the city's postwar prosperity. At the time, nobody in Canada had a better eye or a greater talent for acquisition. The result is an inspiring collection of master works by all the great names of modernist Canadian art, from Maurice Cullen

The Art Gallery of Hamilton on King Street West.

Remnants of stores past still decorate James Street North.

• Art Crawls

The best time to visit the district is during one of its famous Art Crawls, held every second Friday of the month. More than a tour, a Hamilton art crawl is a broadly organized event in which dozens of galleries and community spaces co-ordinate exhibition openings and stage attractions. It has gone on for years and remains remarkably well done. See jamesstreetnorth.ca/blog for schedules of events and exhibitions.

Every September, when the beloved Tiger Cats and fading Argonauts meet in their annual Labour Day Classic, Hamilton's art crawling culminates in

to Emily Carr, with Montreal's Beaver Hall Group well represented along with the more familiar Group of Seven.

The AGH recently renewed its connection to the local creative community by opening a Design Annex, combining exhibition, event and retail space at the head of Hamilton's James Street North arts district, a short walk from the gallery proper.

James Street North

James Street North is a very old, handsome retail district that will remind some of Toronto's Queen West of the late 70s — a burgeoning arts scene existing in apparent harmony with its hard-edged urban surroundings, just before the onslaught of chain stores and fashion boutiques.

CULINARY REVIVAL

There are now enough restaurants on James Street and in the immediate area to support more than one 10-best list on the Internet. The range is broad.

• The colourful **Jack & Lois** diner at the northern end serves creative takes on breakfast and sandwiches.

• The **Berkeley** is the latest addition to the restaurant row taking shape on King William Street, bringing a west-coast atmosphere and menu to Hamilton.

• The **Burnt Tongue**, located at 10 Cannon Street East, is famous for its soups.

• Smoked and barbecued meats at both the **Saltlick Smokehouse** and **Charred** are worth trying.

• **Nabil's Grill**, at the corner of Wilson and James, is universally recommended for their falafel and shawarma.

a festival known as the James Street Supercrawl, which is as refreshingly different from a typical Ontario fall fair as it's possible to get. More than 100,000 people attend the event, which Ontario Tourism named "Tourism Event of the Year" in 2015.

◆ Galleries

At any time, a short walk up James Street from the AGH will bring you to the door of many of the city's most popular galleries.

•   Hamilton Artists Inc., an artist-run enterprise, has held its own at 155 James Street since 1979.

•   Centre [3], also artist-run, at 173 James began as a printmaking studio and is now a full-fledged production, exhibition and education institution.

•   B contemporary at 226 James offers picture framing as well as exhibitions keyed to the Art Crawl.

•   Not precisely on James but well worth a short detour are Gallery 4, located in Hamilton's Central Library at 55 York Boulevard, and the Nathaniel Hughson Art Gallery at 27 John Street North, just east of James.

Keep on walking, and you will find plenty more to see — and plenty to eat — in downtown Hamilton during the heady spring of its revival.

Architecture

Like many other cities across North America, Hamilton's historic core suffered during the 1960s' urban renewal mania, when over 100 buildings were demolished to make room for the

Every second Friday of the month, the Art Crawl takes over James Street North.

The modernist Hamilton City Hall.

RIGHT
The 18-storey Pigott Building is Hamilton's first skyscraper.

Jackson Square shopping centre. The city has, however, begun to make the most of what remains.

Sandyford Place, at the corner of Duke and McNab, is a rare surviving example of a mid-19th-century fine stonework row house built for the rising merchant class of Hamilton. Sandyford Place was the first building designated under the Ontario Heritage Act.

The modernist Hamilton City Hall, an eight-storey, glass, steel-frame building located on Main Street, was designed by city architect Stanley Roscoe and officially opened in 1960. Note the Italian glass tile mosaics forming a band along the exterior.

Another building of note is Hamilton's first skyscraper, the art deco and Gothic revival Pigott Building. Now a condo building, it was built in 1928 and still stands on James Street South.

Interested in more Hamilton architectural history? Historical Hamilton has created a list of buildings and a mobile app. Visit historicalhamilton.com.

SOUTH

Explore the

Royal Botanical Gardens

& THE ESCARPMENT

Nestled at the base of the Niagara Escarpment, downtown Hamilton is not only restoring and repurposing its built landscape, it is beginning to recover some of its natural beauty, including gardens and waterfront spaces. A short trip to the outskirts of the city takes you to a string of stunning waterfalls dotting the escarpment itself.

The Royal Botanical Gardens

Hamilton may still have a ways to go in its effort to rehabilitate the gorgeous geography that once made it such a favoured place for industry, but the

The **RBG Centre**, the year-round focal point of the gardens, houses the Indoor program, the **Greenhouse Café** and a gift shop as well as a two-storey Mediterranean garden. Roses are the main attraction in the adjacent **Hendrie Park**, which also has hiking trails and the **Turner Pavilion Teahouse**.

pioneering Royal Botanical Gardens (RBG) will always be here to show how successful that long game can be. Beginning as a Depression-era make-work project, it's now a major institution that is transforming an entire ecosystem. It's a complex place — part tourist attraction, part research and education institute, part event venue, part conservation area — and spread over a number of non-contiguous sites in Hamilton and Burlington.

◆ The Rock Garden

The one can't-miss experience is the famous Rock Garden — the historic heart of the RBG, which was built almost a century ago in a worked-out gravel pit — when its colours are at their height in early May.

Always a jewel, the Rock Garden recently underwent a major renovation and emerged more sparkling than ever. But don't expect the spectacular drifts of tulips the RBG once planted every

The **Laking Garden**, known for its displays of irises, peonies and clematis, is located just east of the Rock Garden on Plains Road.

The Rock Garden in full bloom.

fall, 100,000 at a time, only to dig them up when they had finished blooming. The new Rock Garden has adopted more sustainable practices, emphasizing native species and year-round visual appeal. The renovation added 28,000 plants of 750 different species to the mix and thoroughly upgraded all the pathways and facilities. There is also an elegant new visitors' centre on the tablelands above the grotto. Find the Rock Garden at 1185 York Boulevard.

Winter at Cootes Paradise Marsh.

◆ Cootes Paradise Marsh

For most of the past century, Cootes Paradise was the opposite of what its name promised. But careful management and restoration by the RBG is bringing it back, and bald eagles now nest on the wooded heights above the water. The former Captain Cootes Trail along the north shore has been renamed Anishinaabe waadiziwin in honour of the area's original inhabitants, and it includes interpretative features that focus on the traditional medicinal plants found in the area. It begins at the RBG Nature Interpretation Centre and is accessible from Old Guelph Road.

There are more trails on the south shore, beginning from Princess Point in the Hamilton neighbourhood of Westdale, where there is also a canoe launch.

◆ The Fishway

The most intriguing sight in the Westdale neighbourhood, located at the outlet of Cootes Paradise March, is the Fishway, a barrier across the channel between the marsh and Hamilton Harbour. The Fishway has dramatically improved the marsh by excluding invasive carp while letting native fish pass. You can see it lifting and sorting trapped fish every day during the spring at 2 p.m.

TREES, PLEASE

Not to be overlooked is the large **Arboretum** at 16 Old Guelph Road, home to a diversity of tree species. Cherries, dogwoods, magnolias and redbuds add to the spring display, and fall colours are also beautiful here. Don't miss the **lilac dell** or **Rasberry House** and its adjacent silo. The arboretum also includes a section devoted to the trees and shrubs native to this area.

and on Mondays, Wednesdays and Fridays during the summer months. To find the Fishway, follow the Desjardins Trail either south from the Arboretum or north from Princess Point.

The Waterfalls

Toronto cherishes its ravines and valleys, but for sheer natural beauty it has nothing to rival its overlooked sibling at the head of the lake. And nothing exemplifies Hamilton's beauty better than the diadem of sparkling waterfalls that tumble over the Niagara Escarpment (a UNESCO world biosphere site) as it circles the city. Local authorities have counted more than 100 of them within city limits, leading some to dub Hamilton — despite Niagara just to the east — the "waterfall capital of the world."

Most of the waterfalls in Hamilton are located along the Bruce Trail and can require anywhere from minimal walking from a nearby parking lot to a long-distance hike to access. Some are accessible by bike. If you are planning to cycle or hike, don't forget to pack snacks and water (and take your garbage out with you). You can find detailed maps for all of Hamilton's waterfalls at waterfalls.hamilton.ca.

RELAX AND RECOUP IN DUNDAS

The lovely town of **Dundas** is lucky it lost out to nearby Hamilton in the great 19th-century race to industrialize. Its relative decline has transformed it into a kind of anti-Hamilton, a sleeping beauty quietly nestled into its own deep green valley and unruffled by the busy world all around it. Because it is almost completely surrounded by conservation lands, Dundas is uniquely free of the commercial sprawl that afflicts most Ontario towns and cities. The result is a relaxing place to recover from the rigors of a hike. A stroll down **King Street** reveals some of the best shopping in the Hamilton region, thriving as a traditional, open-air alternative to the big-box experience that otherwise dominates the retail environment. In addition to shopping, you can check out these other Dundas highlights:

- The **Carnegie Gallery** at 10 King West is a not-for-profit artist-run gallery and gift shop in the 1910 Beaux-Arts style Andrew Carnegie Library building, which was once the town's public library.

- **Bangkok Spoon** at 57 King Street West has authentic, tasty Thai cuisine. It's open for lunch and dinner.

- Go to **Detour Coffee Roasters** for a thoughtfully chosen selection of coffees roasted in their green sustainable roaster. They also serve food in their café at 41 King Street West.

- If you are planning a trip in early June, you might catch the **Dundas International Buskerfest**. See dundasbuskerfest.ca for details.

Tew Falls.

LEFT
Webster Falls.

◆ Two in One: Webster Falls and Tew Falls

Two of the tallest and prettiest falls can be visited in a single hike along the valley of Spencer Creek near the village of Greensville. Dubbed the Spencer Adventure by the Hamilton Conservation Authority, this hike doubles as a journey to the pioneer roots of the Steel City's industrial economy and, perhaps, to its future as well, one in which its "dark Satanic mills," as William Blake described the mills of the Industrial Revolution, have been reduced to picturesque ruins and all is green and pleasant once again.

To access Webster and Tew Falls, begin at Crooks' Hollow Conservation Area. You can follow the trail a few hundred metres upstream to visit the ruins of the 1813 Darnley Grist Mill before heading back down toward the falls.

WEBSTER FALLS

The trail begins in Crooks' Hollow, the cradle of Upper Canadian industry, bustling in the 1820s but identifiable today only by the ruins of a single stone mill beside a narrow country road. Named for James Crooks, the pioneer entrepreneur who developed

HIKE TO DUNDAS PEAK

From Tew Falls, the balance of the **Crooks' Trail** hike follows the rim of the gorge until it terminates at **Dundas Peak**, a famous lookout with terrific views back up the gorge in one direction and out over the open lake in the other. The route from **Crooks' Hollow** to the peak is a little over 5 kilometres, making for an 11-kilometre round trip if done in one go.

 Protect yourself and the environment: The slopes and edges of the escarpment can be unstable. Keep to marked trails at all times, not only for your own safety, but to protect the many rare and sensitive plants and animals that call this area home.

it, the village was the site of a dozen enterprises drawing power from the creek, including Canada's first paper mill, built for Crooks by a family of Irish stonemasons named Barber. Traces of the early mills and factories are scattered along the trail as it follows the creek downstream, through the Crooks' Hollow Conservation Area, to the brink of the escarpment at Webster Falls.

This is one of the best known and most accessible of all of Hamilton's waterfalls, which means it can be crowded on weekends. Parking is limited and enforcement vigilant, so walking down from Crooks' Hollow is always the best bet. But once you arrive, you'll understand the fuss. Webster Falls is a perfect postcard at any time of year.

TEW FALLS

From Webster Falls the hike joins the Bruce Trail and continues a few kilometres through the Spencer Gorge to the even taller Tew Falls. Fed by the barest trickle of water from Logie's Creek, Tew is a "ribbon falls" that descends 41 metres — almost as high as Niagara itself — into a giant limestone bowl at the head of the gorge. The size of the bowl suggests there was once a Niagara-sized flow over this ledge. Unlike Webster Falls, Tew can dry up in the summer.

◆ More Falls by Car, Bike or Hike

Dedicated explorers could easily spend a weekend rushing from one waterfall to another along the rim of the escarpment in Hamilton, but a few side trips will be enough to satisfy most.

• Starting in central Hamilton at the south end of Dundurn Street, the 2.7-kilometre Chedoke Radial Trail passes several falls as it leads toward Ancaster and the Dundas Valley. This is a flat trail, if you want to cycle.

• Another cluster of popular waterfalls is located at the head of the Red Hill Creek Valley in eastern Hamilton, which you can explore by walking the Bruce Trail along the brow of the mountain. Access the Red Hill Trail from Red Hill Valley Parkway by exiting at Dartnell Road. Turn east (left) onto Stonechurch Road East and left again onto Pritchard Road until you reach a T intersection. There is a parking lot just to the east.

• If you are energetic, you can reach Buttermilk Falls, Albion Falls and others from downtown Hamilton by cycling or hiking the 9.5-kilometre Escarpment Rail Trail. If driving, exit the Red Hill Valley Parkway South at Stone Church Road East. Turn right onto Pritchard Road, and then left onto Mud Street. Continue onto Mountain Brow Boulevard. Park in the parking lot on the right after Limeridge Road East. Follow the trail to the waterfall lookout. For safety reasons the gorge around the falls is now fenced off, but you can still enjoy the falls from a safe distance along marked trails.

• The Devil's Punchbowl, just a little bit east of Albion Falls, is one of the region's most spectacular falls. You'll also get a chance to drive or ride one of Hamilton's most scenic routes, Ridge Road, which runs along the brow of the mountain toward Niagara. To get there from Albion Falls, follow Mud Street east to Centennial Parkway (Road 20), turn north on 20 and then west onto Ridge Road.

LEFT
Albion Falls.

The Devil's Punchbowl.

SOUTH

Uncover

Hamilton

HISTORY & HERITAGE

It is sobering to consider how much less fun our world would be absent the activities of older men obsessed with obsolete technology. Thanks to their efforts, steam engines of all kinds, water-powered sawmills, vintage race cars, tractors, wooden ships and ancient airplanes all continue to chuff, roar and fly. The result is an entire network of interesting, often eccentric attractions spread throughout the countryside.

Canadian Warplane Heritage Museum

None of these attractions is bigger or closer to spectacular than the Canadian Warplane Heritage Museum.

Beginning with the impulsive decision of two veteran pilots to buy a single WWII fighter — the one in which museum co-founder Alan Ness ultimately lost his life in a 1977 crash at the CNE air show — the collection has grown to comprise more than 40 aircraft, most of them restored to flying condition and housed in a vast, purpose-built building. Trainers, fighters

and bombers are all represented, with pride of place going to the museum's painstakingly restored Avro Lancaster night bomber, made in Malton and one of only two in the world still flying. Museum members have the option of booking flights on a dozen different aircraft, from a biplane trainer to a B-52 bomber — and including the Lancaster, which completed a trans-Atlantic flight to Britain for a reunion with its fellow survivor in 2014.

Several of the aircraft have viewing stands so you can see right inside the cockpits, and kids in particular will enjoy taking the controls of the flight simulators that are free with the price of admission.

Open year-round seven days a week, the museum is located adjacent to Hamilton Airport just south of the city. Parking is free, and the museum's

kid-friendly café (open for breakfast and lunch) and gift shop are open daily.

The Royal Canadian Navy destroyer *Haida*

It would almost be wrong to visit the warplane museum without also stopping to visit Hamilton's greatest living war memorial, the Royal Canadian Navy destroyer *Haida*, now

The restored Avro Lancaster is a highlight of the Warplane Museum.

ABOVE
The exterior of the Canadian Warplane Heritage Museum.

the centrepiece of the city's slowly reviving waterfront. Dubbed "Canada's fightingest warship," she is also the luckiest, having lost only two men over a 20-year career engaged in dozens of battles on three oceans over two wars. Long docked at the Toronto waterfront after being decommissioned in the 1960s, *Haida* was rusting and neglected when Hamilton MP Sheila Copps arranged to have her towed across the lake and docked. Now a museum and National Historic Site operated by Parks Canada, *Haida* is back in top condition and more accessible than ever. Once aboard, you can tour the decks on your own or take one of a number of different guided tours that lead into every secret cranny of the old warship.

The *Haida* is docked on the Hamilton waterfront near Bayfront Park. You can walk to it along James Street North from the GO station.

RIGHT
The exterior of the Hamilton Museum of Steam and Technology.

The Royal Canadian Navy destroyer *Haida*.

Hamilton Museum of Steam and Technology
The Hamilton Waterworks not only stands as a nationally significant monument, it survives today as an almost-perfect small museum.

◆ September 1860
"Who living in Canada had not heard of the Hamilton Waterworks?" a proud local reporter queried in September 1860, as a teenaged Prince of Wales, the future King Edward VII, ceremonially turned the valve that started the pump that, for the first time, brought fresh lake water to the cholera-stricken town.

To Canadians of the day, this compact powerhouse and the mighty steam engines it enclosed were no mere infrastructure: Designed and built entirely by a Canadian engineer and local manufacturers, it was both a life-saving miracle of modern technology and a major achievement in the transformation of the

young colony from an agrarian back-water into a modern industrial nation. They knew what they were seeing, and their pride was fitting.

◆ A Century and a Half Later

These days, nobody seems to have heard of the Hamilton Waterworks, now known as the Hamilton Museum of Steam and Technology. It sits isolated and overlooked as the world it helped create speeds by heedlessly on the city's east-end expressways. But those who stop to visit will discover what the Victorian hoopla was about.

The museum's importance may not be immediately apparent to visitors as they first encounter this handsome brick complex and enter through the old boiler room, with its conventional in-formation panels and ancillary exhibits, but stepping through to the adjoining pumphouse is a stupendous experience.

Quite apart from the fact that it contains a matched pair of the largest antique steam engines in existence, bordered by cast-iron flywheels standing three storeys tall and topped by two carefully balanced 13-tonne "walking beams," this is no mere engine room. Built as a high-visibility showpiece of local engineering talent, it remains one

Do you or your kids need to kick back or let off some steam after the museums? Pack a picnic ahead of time and lunch at **Confederation Beach Park**, enjoy a hike along the park's 4.5-kilometre promenade or try the **Adventure Village**'s go-karts, batting cages or minigolf. **Hutch's** along the beach offers fish and chips, hot dogs and hamburgers.

of the most architecturally dramatic interiors in the country.

The pumphouse and its engines are so closely interlocked, with such tight clearances between the parts that move and those that don't, that exploring the multi-level galleries feels like walking inside the machine itself. The climax comes when museum staff spin up the massive flywheel of the north engine with a retrofitted electric motor and the whole apparatus comes smoothly alive, beam rocking and pistons plunging, with only the hiss and heat of steam missing to complete the perfect illusion of time travel back to the Victorian era.

DUNDURN CASTLE

Dundurn Castle, an Italianate villa built in the 1830s, was home to railway magnate, lawyer and premier of Upper Canada Sir Allan Napier and his family. Admission is very affordable and includes a guided tour, entrance to the military museum on site and access to the restored kitchen garden.

Ship-spot on the Welland Canal

A freighter is docked in Welland Canal's Lock 3.

Dedicated ship-spotters (which includes just about all young kids!) will love to spend the day visiting the Welland Canal. The rest of us would be remiss to overlook it during any trip to Niagara.

It's always stupendous to stand a few metres away from huge ocean-going ships as they slide quietly past and

For some home-style Italian comfort food in Welland, try **Don Marco's Italian Eatery** at 248 Wellington Street.

begin to climb a 100-metre bluff up a "flight" of locks cut like a giant staircase straight up the escarpment, lifted by gravity alone. The ships fill the locks with mere centimetres of clearance on either side and loom overhead like tall buildings. They are stately and mesmerizing. "At Niagara Falls I need about 20 minutes," one British tourist commented on TripAdvisor, "but at the Canal I can spend a day."

Given that the Welland Canal has been subjected to repeated terrorist attacks going back to the early 19th century, it remains amazingly accessible to gawkers today. There are two officially designated "viewing complexes," one at Lock 3, where northbound ships

begin the ascent of the escarpment, and another at Lock 7, the last step of the climb.

If you're clever, you can time your visit to ensure the close sight of passing ships by going to greatlakes-seaway.com and clicking on the Seaway map, which provides real-time information about the position and direction of all ships in the canal.

A freighter passes under a lift bridge along the Welland Canal.

CYCLE THE WELLAND CANAL
The **Welland Canal Trail** gives an intimate view of the shipping action, running 42 kilometres down the west bank of the canal and passing through the little-visited towns of **Thorold**, **Welland** and **Port Colborne**. Uniquely in the region, the paved route is entirely car-free, making it a favourite with locals and safe for kids.

The viewing platform at the Welland Canals Centre.

Welland Canals Centre

There may be more compelling attractions in southern Ontario, but there is none as weirdly eclectic as the group assembled at the Welland Canals Centre at Lock 3.

Here, you can admire ships up close from an elevated viewing platform and view a scale model showing the workings of the canal and detailed information about its history since 1829. You can also dive deep into the story of Canada's original national

sport at the Ontario Lacrosse Hall of Fame and Museum and learn about the Underground Railroad and local Black history at an award-winning exhibit called Follow the North Star at the St. Catharines Museum.

PORT COLBORNE HISTORICAL AND MARINE MUSEUM AND HERITAGE VILLAGE

A 25-minute drive south will take you to **Port Colborne** and its museum and heritage village: a collection of buildings and gardens, including a pavilion and picnic tables, where you can eat a packed lunch. Or plan ahead to ensure **Arabella's Tea Room** at 61 Princess Street is open, so you can enjoy tea, biscuits and preserves. The **Historical and Marine Museum** highlights the Welland Canal and includes marine artifacts.

SOUTH

Visit

Niagara Falls

At the time of writing, the website TripAdvisor has posted some 87,387 reviews of "Things to Do" in Niagara Falls, including 22,100 reviews of the falls themselves and 39,800 photos. Here's one more number: 14 million visitors a year. Add that up, and you get one of the world's most outrageous tourist traps. But it's one that rarely disappoints.

Nobody has ever said "meh" to Niagara Falls. It is the only attraction anywhere near Toronto that truly qualifies as "must see" — especially if the ones doing the seeing are children.

And seen through the eyes of a child, if you can still manage that, the surrounding trap can be fun. It's the closest thing we have to Las Vegas, Canadian-style, in a spectacular natural setting.

But don't expect just to fall out of your car and start swinging the selfie stick out over Table Rock. While it's possible to park within walking distance of the falls (early in the morning on a rainy weekday), you are far more likely to be relegated to a distant lot served by crowded shuttle buses. And with high-season traffic that can rival Toronto's, driving here is no fun at all.

No matter how many times you visit, the falls are a spectacular sight to see.

Hop on a Bus or Book a Charter Tour

There is no day-trip destination out of Toronto better served by public transportation. Buses are cheap and run all the time. Greyhound, Coach Canada, Megabus and GO all run scheduled services. Entire fleets of motor coaches surge through downtown Toronto every morning, picking up Niagara-bound tourists at all the major hotels and returning en masse to drop them off in the evening. (Niagara bus tours are the reverse of a local secret known only to insiders: They're well-known to every tourist who has ever stopped here for more than a night, but still mysterious to native Torontonians.)

CLIFTON HILL FAVOURITES

If you are determined to enjoy the legendary tackiness of Clifton Hill, don't miss these classics:

- The Great Canadian Midway (a kid version of the casino!)
- Guinness World Records Museum
- Louis Tussaud's Waxworks
- The Niagara Skywheel

The standard tour offered by all companies includes visits to the falls, Niagara-on-the-Lake and a winery. The most popular upgrade is a trip on a Hornblower catamaran — successor to the *Maid of the Mist* — followed by lunch or a ticket to the Skylon Tower. Prices range from as little as $70 to more than $150 for tours with all the options. Guides are certified for local knowledge by the Niagara Parks Commission.

You could show up in virtually any downtown Toronto lobby at eight in the morning and book a tour, but it's always cheaper to book online in advance. In any case, there couldn't be an easier way to visit the falls.

• Charter Bus Tour Options

Some of the best and most convenient deals are available from charter bus companies.

• Safeway Tours offers free round trips (for gamblers only) to Fallsview Casino from two dozen GTA locations. See safewaytours.net/en/casino-tours.

• King Tours operates five different excursions from Toronto, ranging from a falls-only tour to an all-inclusive package that includes a Hornblower boat trip, lunch and a wine tasting. King also runs tours departing from Markham, Mississauga and Brampton. See kingtours.ca.

• Zoom Tours offers five different day and evening bus package tours to the falls. See niagarafallsbustours.ca.

• Airlink Niagara Bus Tours charges a little more than average for its tour, but the price includes a boat tour and lunch. See niagarabustour.com.

Some tour companies take visitors straight to Fallsview Casino.

ABOVE
Tour buses can get visitors right in the middle of the action.

The Hornblower catamaran as it heads back from Horseshoe Falls.

• Niagara Falls Day Tours boasts a certificate of excellence from TripAdvisor. See niagaratorontotours.com.
• For slightly less expensive tours, try City Sightseeing Toronto (citysightseeingtoronto.com) and BEST Toronto Tours (myniagaratours.com).

Niagara Falls Attractions

It costs nothing to enjoy a close view of one of the world's most magnificent cataracts, but a few steps in any direction can be ruinously expensive, even before you enter the lavish Fallsview Casino. If you plan to visit a number of attractions, it makes sense to buy an Adventure Pass at niagaraparks.com; different packages are available, and they all include use of WEGO, the hop-on, hop-off shuttle bus system for Niagara's tourist areas.

If you only have time or money for one attraction, choose Hornblower Niagara Cruises, located at 5920 Niagara Parkway. Successor to the company that operated successive *Maid of the Mist* tours of the falls from 1846 to 2013, Hornblower runs two 700-passenger catamarans on the dramatic 20-minute route to the foot of the falls and back. The new operation is slick and the experience — as ever — is unforgettable.

SOUTH

Cycle the Niagara Region

BIKE TRAIN ROUTES

There is no more interesting or congenial region for cycling in Ontario than Niagara. Niagara was early to realize the potential of cycle tourism, and the result is the province's most developed support system for the activity. This is a place where "bike friendly" is becoming big business.

The GO Bike Train Service

Civilization advanced one solid step in the first decade of the 21st century when GO Transit introduced Bike Train service to the Niagara region.

The GO Bike Train service is a great way to enjoy cycling outside of Toronto.

The Niagara River Recreation Trail is a devoted bike path, making it a safer alternative to the Niagara Parkway.

There may be easier ways to get there and get around, but none is more flexible or fun for those willing to make a small effort. It's a pleasure in itself to make the entire trip, taking in as many attractions as one may like, without enduring the dreaded QEW or even once stepping into a car or bus.

The GO Bike Train is a seasonal service, operating on weekends and holidays from Victoria Day until Thanksgiving. Leaving from Union Station, it stops at Exhibition, Port Credit, Oakville, Burlington, St. Catharines and Niagara Falls. There is no need to box or bag your bicycle, and the trip takes about two hours each way.

The Routes

As for routes, there are so many possibilities that choosing one can be daunting. The Niagara Freewheelers Bicycle Touring Club has mapped more than 500 options on its website, thefreewheelers.com. Below are two that show Niagara at its best while making the most of the Bike Train connection.

NAVIGATION

An abundance of on-road signage and easily available maps make life easy for cyclists in Niagara. The **Niagara Cycling Tourism Centre** (niagaracyclingtourism.com) publishes an excellent map on waterproof paper that is available from the tourist information centres in either Niagara Falls or NOTL. (The downloadable version is too small to be of much use.) For venturing east of the peninsula on the Greenbelt Route, you'll need to consult the maps published at greenbelt.ca and waterfronttrail.org. For connections between those two systems, see the maps published at hamilton.ca/cycling.

◆ The Lesser Niagara Circle Route

The region's signature route, the Greater Niagara Circle, is too long for most casual cyclists and leaves little room for sightseeing. But a truncated version — let's call it the Lesser Niagara Circle Route — is the one ride everybody should do. It follows mainly gentle terrain in the northeast quadrant of the peninsula, climbs the escarpment only once and passes virtually every popular attraction. At about 60 kilometres, it's easily rideable in a day, but it could take a week to ride if you stopped to explore everything along the way.

From the Niagara Falls train station, ride east two blocks to the Niagara Parkway, which follows the west bank of the river 56 kilometres from Lake Erie to Lake Ontario. On this route, the falls are a side trip, located 3 kilometres to the south. But take care: there are no bike lanes, and traffic near the falls can be heavy.

To follow the circle, ride north on the Niagara Parkway toward Niagara-on-the-Lake, 20 kilometres away on one of the oldest roads in Ontario, the portage around the falls. Three-quarters of a century ago, Sir Winston Churchill dubbed this parkway "the prettiest Sunday afternoon drive in the world," and it's even prettier on two wheels. Safer, too: north of the gorge, the bike path separates onto its own right-of-way, the Niagara River Recreation Trail.

The parkway is also rife with roadside attractions, including the White Water Walk deep in the gorge, along with the Whirlpool Rapids; the village of Queenston (see pages 102–6); and some of the oldest vineyards in the

Think about packing a lunch and picnicking along the route. That way, you have more time to enjoy the ride. Don't forget plenty of water, too!

WHITE WATER WALK
Travel by elevator to the base of the gorge to observe the ancient rock layers and crashing white-water waves as you walk the short boardwalk. Along the way, there are several viewing platforms that allow you to see the **Whirlpool Rapids** up close. This is one of the more affordable Niagara attractions and is located at 4330 River Road (Niagara Parkway).

region, owned by such pioneer wineries as Inniskillin, Reif Estates and Peller Estates. But if you only have time for one or two stops, consider making the Butterfly Conservatory one of them. It's a magical place, and the perfect antidote to the hubbub of the falls. You'll find it on the west side of the road, 3 kilometres north of the Whirlpool.

Niagara-on-the-Lake is its own world, well worth a day of its own (see pages 112–7). But to complete the circle, follow the Waterfront Trail along Lakeshore Road west to the mouth of the Welland Canal at Port Weller. Cross the Lock 1 lift bridge, turn south onto the canal bike trail and ride alongside the hulking lakers and "salties" until you pass under the impressive Garden City Skyway. This is the point the route diverts from the Greater Niagara Circle Route. After the underpass, dodge back east over the canal on Road 81, take the first left onto Niagara Stone Road (Road 55) and then the

first right (east) onto quiet Queenston Road. This puts you on the Greenbelt Route, which runs under the brow of the escarpment through the village of St. David's and onto York Road into Queenston. From there, it's one good climb and 10 kilometres back south along the parkway to Niagara Falls.

The Niagara Greenbelt Route

This route is more challenging than the Lesser Niagara Circle Route, and it forgoes sightseeing in favour of a long, scenic traverse of the peninsula from east to west along the opening section of the Greenbelt Route. It starts at Niagara Falls and ends just over

No matter which of the two routes you choose, you'll go through the historic village of **St. David's**. Stop by **Ravine Vineyard Estate Winery** at 1366 York Road to enjoy the vineyard, winery, kitchen garden and a delicious meal.

THE BUTTERFLY CONSERVATORY

Southern Ontario is nobody's idea of a tropical paradise, but the **Niagara Parks Botanical Gardens**, located at 2565 Niagara Parkway, has created a convincing pocket-sized version under glass at its delightful **Butterfly Conservatory**. Thousands of butterflies of 45 different species fly freely through the elegant space, which is lushly planted and networked with walking paths for visitors. If you've already experienced the crush at the falls, a visit here will be welcome respite. The **Butterfly Café** is usually less crowded than similar eateries closer to the falls.

90 kilometres later at Burlington, where the Bike Train stops on the way home to Toronto. The route used to be lined wall-to-wall with peach orchards that are magnificent in the spring. Now it's all vines, along with some of Niagara's most prestigious wineries tucked into the benchlands beneath the brow of the escarpment, including Malivoire, Cave Springs and Thirty Bench.

Follow the Lesser Niagara Circle Route from Niagara Falls train station to Queenston. Ride west from Queenston along York Road, and just past St. David's turn right onto Queenston Road. Ride over the Welland Canal and through St. Catharines (west along Queenston Street and then south on St. Paul Street). From St. Catharines, follow King Street (Road 81) west toward the quaint village of Jordan and the picturesque Twenty Valley wine region. The tour climbs the escarpment over the even prettier Beamsville Bench, a top sub-appellation region with some impressive wineries. Past Beamsville, turn left on Lincoln Avenue, and ride south and then west to Mountainview Road. Turn left on Mountainview and follow it until you hit Thirty Road. Ride Thirty Road north, and then veer west (left) onto Ridge Road. Follow Ridge Road on the brow of the mountain overlooking Hamilton, a truly spectacular entrance to the city. From there, you leave the Greenbelt Route and

drop down the Red Hill Valley to meet the Waterfront Trail at Confederation Park. The Burlington train station is 12 kilometres to the north, across the bay. Leave the Waterfront Trail at Brant Street and follow Brant until you hit Fairview Street. Turn right and Burlington train station will be a few hundred metres on the left.

Both routes pass through the south's lovely wine country.

If you are making good time, stop by the **Jordan House Tavern** just off King Street in Jordan. The tavern's upscale sister property, **Inn on the Twenty**, located at the Cave Springs Winery, remains one of Niagara's premier culinary destinations.

SOUTH

Spend a day in

Queenston Heights

A monument to Major-General Sir Isaac Brock stands in Queenston Heights Park.

Explore the site and surroundings of one of Canada's most famous battles.

A Picnic in the Park

Picnicking at Queenston Heights Park atop the escarpment on a summer Sunday is like stepping into a *plein-air* Impressionist painting. You lounge in the dappled shade while children run free on the grass, kites fly and Niagara's own Sgt. Pepper conducts the musical entertainment from his blossom-fringed bandstand. Nothing in dear old Ontario could rival the

experience for sheer, startling whole-
someness.

That such scenes take place on one
of the country's bloodiest battlefields
only adds to their interest — on
every side there are memorials and
monuments, all dominated by the
towering column supporting a statue
of Major-General Sir Isaac Brock, the
hero of infant Upper Canada, who
died in the famous 1812 battle that
pushed American invaders back across
the frontier.

There are two dozen plaques and
markers commemorating the great
battle throughout the park, including
a self-guided five-station walking

tour installed by Parks Canada. The
latest memorial to join the group is
Landscape of Nations, which commemorates the role of Indigenous

Major John Norton
(Teyoninhokarawen)
stands as a sentry
at the entrance of
the Landscape of
Nations memorial.

 The view of the great river
below is worth the climb up
the claustrophobic spiral
staircase inside the tower
of 150-year-old **Major-
General Sir Isaac Brock
monument**, which tightens
ominously as it winds to
the top — a must-do for
all enterprising children.
An interpretive program is
offered daily.

Queenston Heights Park includes two picnic pavilions, washrooms, a playground with splash pad and a snack bar.

warriors, mainly Haudenosaunee (also known as the Iroquois), who played a conspicuous role in helping British soldiers and Canadian militia repel the invaders. Built within the grassy remains of an 1812 artillery battery, it's an impressive experience that adds a long-missing chapter to the usual school-book history of these almost mythological events.

A different band plays in the bandshell every Sunday afternoon throughout the warm months. Arrive early if you're driving, as parking can be scarce.

A Walk through the Village

No matter how crowded the Heights become, the tiny, perfect village in their shadow retains an almost magical poise. A few very old blocks of settlement set just apart from the Niagara Parkway, Queenston always rewards a

visitor. A footpath leads down from the Heights. Once a busy hub at the foot of the long portage that circumvented the famous falls, Queenston somehow manages to stay well off the beaten track that speeds right past it. Canadian history runs thick here.

There is no more an iconic sight than the real-life homestead of the almost mythical War of 1812 hero Laura Secord, which has been polished to rustic perfection by the Niagara Parks. Guided tours are provided by qualified costumed interpreters, and Laura Secord chocolates are available. Find the homestead at 29 Queenston Street.

At the north end of the village stands Willowbank, an 1830s mansion built in a grand neoclassic style more associated with the antebellum South than humble Upper Canada. It operates today as the headquarters of a private, non-profit school for heritage conservation and ecological development. You can see it standing proudly on its hill, Tara-like, from a vantage point on

QUEENSTON HEIGHTS RESTAURANT
Not up for brown-bagging it? Queenston Heights Restaurant, right in the park, offers reasonably priced fresh food. Best of all is the restaurant's magnificent view of the wide Niagara River as it winds north toward Lake Ontario. The restaurant is open seasonally; call **(905) 262-4274** for reservations.

Queenston Street at the intersection of Dee Road. A bit farther north brings you to the private RiverBrink Art Museum, which specializes in early Canadiana.

Mackenzie Printery

When a group of local printing enthusiasts went looking for a place to house their collection of old presses in the 1980s, good luck brought them to this elegant stone building at 1 Queenston Street, at the foot of Queenston Heights. Lovely digs in any case, the fact that it was once the home of pioneer newspaper publisher and rebel leader William Lyon Mackenzie made it an especially apt location. Although Mackenzie lived here for less than a year before leaving for Muddy York, the provincial capital, this is where he published the first numbers of his rabble-rousing newspaper, the *Colonial Advocate*. Stung by its unrelenting attacks, Mackenzie's elite opponents in the Family Compact destroyed his press and threw the remains into Toronto Bay. His successful prosecution of the perpetrators helped to firmly establish press freedom in Canada.

Until some future archaeologist dredges some old pieces of the Mackenzie press out of the silt at the foot of Yonge Street, pride of place at this museum goes to the extremely rare Louis Roy press, named for the printer who produced the first government proclamations in 18th-century Upper Canada. One of seven surviving wooden presses in the world, it was used to print the 1793 *Act Against Slavery*, which outlawed slavery in the province.

The view of Willowbank from Queenston Street.

LEFT
Laura Secord's restored homestead.

A dozen other more-or-less antique machines fill the museum, including a working Linotype, a 20th-century workhorse that drank hot lead and spit out the news line by line. There are no barriers here, no glass cases: everything's in the open for touching and trying. The printery prides itself on being "the best hands-on museum in Upper Canada," where guests can learn how to set moveable type and operate two heritage printing presses.

ABOVE
The stony exterior of the Mackenzie Printery.

The museum's Louis Roy press.

Drink in the Niagara Wine Region

From Niagara-on-the-Lake to St. Catharines, the Niagara wine region is home to hectares and hectares of vineyards producing stellar wines in a picture-perfect countryside setting.

For anyone old enough to remember when domestic wine sold for a dollar a bottle, and only to the most unfortunate alcoholics, the emergence of the Niagara wine region is miraculous. Niagara wines today are not only enjoyed around the world, they are the foundation of the most successful new tourist industry in Canada. Niagara wineries are second only to the

The peninsula's climate and soil make it ideal for growing grapes.

Fields of vines now dominate the region's landscape.

neighbouring falls as an Ontario tourist destination.

One result is that the Niagara Wine Route is now a well-beaten path. (And given the two activities it was designed to encourage — drinking and driving — it remains one of the more dubious promotions devised for the region.) It's also a maze: With more than 100 separate wineries now spread throughout the peninsula, every road is a wine route. Adding to the complications, each winery has its own hours and protocol; some offer tours, some tasting or dining, with or without

reservations, and so on. But planning ahead and finding the best approach will make it worth it in the end.

Go It Alone or Get Help?

There are two ways to tackle the problem of enjoying Niagara wine on its own *terroir*.

1. Do it yourself: Recruit a designated driver and lay out a detailed plan of attack. The website winecountryontario.ca has some truly helpful tools in that regard, including an interactive route planner connecting more than 80 local wineries, descriptions

of each one, and an archive of articles documenting the experiences of expert wine tourists. If you are planning your own tour, consider confining your route to one of the two distinct regional appellations in Niagara, either the wineries of the Escarpment region west of St. Catharines or those of Niagara-on-the-Lake to the east. You'll do more tasting and less travelling.

2. Take an organized wine tour: This is the easier and increasingly popular option. There are now so many tours that choosing one can be as difficult as finding the right wineries on your own.

Despite that, many high-season tours sell out early and need to be booked well in advance. But competition is keen, prices are reasonable, and logistics are never an issue. Most offer a complimentary pick-up and drop-off service at all local hostelries. It really is the way to go. See the next two pages for some standout tour options.

Niagara's wine country is the second biggest draw to the region.

WINE TOUR OPTIONS

Niagara Vintage Wine Tours is a large operation that runs seven days a week, year round, offering a dozen different packages, from half-day wine-and-cheese jaunts to full-on culinary extravaganzas. TripAdvisor ranks it first among 66 entries for "Food & Drink Tours in Niagara-on-the-Lake." See niagaravintagewinetours.com for bookings.

Crush on Niagara Wine Tours, one of the original companies to offer wine tours of the peninsula, caters to enthusiasts with a variety of "sommelier created winespired journeys," including several that explore the Twenty Valley west of St. Catharines. Owner Andrew Brooks, a sommelier and winery owner himself, wrote a book on this trade, *Crush on Niagara: The Definitive Wine Tour Guide*. See crushtours.com.

Magnificent Tours, which calls itself Niagara's largest tour company, runs a relatively inexpensive half-day tasting tour of Niagara-on-the-Lake wineries for people staying in the big hotels in Niagara Falls. See magnificentniagarafallstours.com.

Winery Tours of Niagara is a highly rated service offering five different daily tours, mostly around the eastern peninsula. If you're not staying overnight at one of the designated pick-up locations, the company has arranged for free parking at the Hilton Garden Inn, 500 York Road in Niagara-on-the-Lake. See winerytoursofniagara.com.

Grape and Wine Tours provide the usual assortment of tour options, with one twist: the "Via Rail Express Lunch Fiesta Tour," which picks up passengers from Toronto or Oakville at the Niagara Falls train station in the morning and drops them off in time to catch the evening train home. For those who drive, the company provides free parking at its Niagara-on-the-Lake base. See grapeandwinetours.com.

The Vintage Hotel Group, which has long dominated the accommodation and dining scene in Niagara-on-the-Lake, operates daily tours in an old-fashioned trolley twice a day from various locations in the village. It's a quick jaunt, visiting two wineries and lasting three hours. See vintage-hotels.com.

Niagara Wine Tour Guides takes a populist approach, promising entertaining guides and even junk-food pairings in its tours. They like to start early to beat the crowds, taking small groups to some of the region's smaller wineries. See niagarawinetourguides.com

While some companies use sleek German vans for private tours, only the **Community Transport Group** chauffeurs wine tourists in a classic London black cab. See ctgcanada.ca.

WINE TOURS BY BIKE

Niagara Wine Tours International is one of the few companies catering to tourists who prefer bicycles over the shuttle buses that normally ply these routes. They offer four different bike tours to wineries on the frontier from their Niagara-on-the-Lake (NOTL) base, ranging in distance from 12 to 29 kilometres. Custom-fitted touring bikes are provided. See niagaraworldwinetours.com.

Zoom Leisure Bikes is a dedicated two-wheel rental operation that also offers four different tours, including one self-guided route. Two kiosks along the Niagara Parkway, as well as a main outlet in downtown NOTL, allow for flexible pick-up and drop-off arrangements. See zoomleisure.com.

Grape Escape Wine Tours is another NOTL company that provides bicycle as well as vehicle tours, with five different two-wheeled tour options, ranging from 15 to 25 kilometres in length. Bike rentals are included. See tourniagarawineries.com.

Niagara Getaway Wine Tours, located just outside NOTL in Virgil, has organized a self-guided bicycle tour that allows people to travel at their own pace while visiting five different wineries in the area. And you won't have to lug any bottles along with you, as the company will pick up what you buy and bring it back to Virgil. See niagaragetaways.com.

Tour Niagara-on-the-Lake

S ay what you will about "Niagara-on-the-Take" — the summer crowds, the belching buses, the suffocating cuteness of Queen Street — this is a fascinating and important place. Not only is it the oldest and best preserved early 19th-century town in the province, Niagara-on-the-Lake (NOTL) is one of the few that truly deserves to be called historic.

Notable NOTL

NOTL is where the refugees from the American Revolution first convened a separate polity called Upper Canada,

Burke House, built in the 1820s, exemplifies the "tasteful plainness" of NOTL's architecture.

The Prince of Wales Hotel.

defended it amid blood and fire, and expressed their ideal of freedom on the new frontier with a defiant gentility. It's like an Upper Canadian Charleston, minus the slave quarters hidden at the bottom of the elegant gardens. Indeed, this town is also where our infant Parliament passed its 1793 *Act Against Slavery*, which abolished the practice in Canada and ultimately transformed the Niagara Peninsula into a major haven for freedom-seeking passengers on the famous Underground Railroad (see pages 123–5 for more information).

Niagara (the hyphenated descriptor came later) was elegant from the beginning, built with "a degree of neatness and taste" that, according to one 18th-century observer, simulated "the garb of wealth and of long-established culture" on the new frontier.

Yankee invaders, aided by dastardly Canadian renegades, burned it to the ground in 1813, but stubborn Niagarans rebuilt their town on the same pattern, competing "to outdo each other in tasteful plainness," according to Katherine Ashenburg, author of *Going to Town: Architectural Walking Tours in Southern Ontario.* As the author notes, "one street back" from Queen transports you into an impeccably preserved historic landscape, with the finest collection of early houses in the province, where "the garb of wealth and of long-established culture" is an illusion no longer.

Walking the Historic Town
◆ Guided Tours

There's a niche for everything touristic in Niagara, and Old Town Tours is here to serve those who want to explore NOTL on their own two feet. The small

Corks Winebar & Eatery at 19 Queen Street, the meeting point for Old Town Tours, has an extensive wine list and selection of beers on tap, and they serve a pub-style lunch and dinner. The patio offers a great place to take in historic Queen Street.

The Court House Theatre.

company offers daily tours for both public and private groups, each lasting about two hours, led by qualified guides well versed in local lore. It's recommended that you book in advance, either online at oldtowntours.ca or by phone at 1-888-492-3532. Make sure to wear sensible shoes and bring rainwear, as tours go rain or shine.

◆ DIY Tour

Most people will be content to make their own tour. Here's an itinerary that makes the most of NOTL over a dozen closely spaced blocks:

1.   Begin at the landmark Prince of Wales Hotel, located with a suitably royal flourish where King and Queen Streets meet.

2.   Kitty corner is the Niagara Apothecary from 1820, which is now a popular small museum.

3.   Walking west toward the clock tower takes you past the town's most distinctive storefronts, especially those on the south side of Queen Street that flank the austere stone courthouse, which dates from 1847 and now houses the Shaw Festival's Court House Theatre. The colourful boutique at No. 16 dates from 1830. The fine brick building at the southeast corner of Regent Street is one of the oldest buildings on Queen Street, built in 1825.

4.   The south side of Queen past Victoria, one block further west, is another harmonious row of commercial buildings dating from the 1830s and 1840s. One of the earliest and most characteristic Loyalist houses in the

town, built soon after the 1813 fire, the Rogers House at the northwest corner of Queen and Gate Streets contains a fireplace mantel that was rescued from an earlier family home on the same site just prior to the 1813 arson. The house is currently a popular B & B.

5. A swing south down Gate and east onto Johnson Street takes you through a living museum of early 19th-century residential architecture.

6. A detour west on Johnson and south onto Simcoe brings you to St. Andrew's Presbyterian Church, the most impressive single building in town, with a bold Greek Temple front in the Yankee style, simulated magnificently in Canadian pine.

7. Walk back east along Centre Street to Victoria and head north past Queen to Prideaux Street. The two blocks of Prideaux leading east to King Street are quintessential Niagara. Turn south on King and you're back where you started.

8. If you want, you can visit another cluster of historic houses by walking south of Queen and east along Platoff Street (named for Matvei Platov, a Cossack hero of the Napoleonic Wars).

9. A 10-minute walk south takes you to Butler's Barracks National Historic Site (see page 116).

10. Another 20 minutes across the commons will take you to another National Historic Site, Fort George (see page 116).

St. Andrew's Presbyterian Church on Simcoe Street.

After your walk, the English-style pub at the **Olde Angel Inn** might appeal to your appetite for food as well as history. Located at 224 Regent Street, Ontario's oldest operating inn was established in 1789 and rebuilt in 1815, after the War of 1812. Each of the three dining rooms comes with a cozy gas fireplace.

Military Manoeuvres
◆ Butler's Barracks

The four straightforward clapboard buildings set serenely in a shady park at the foot of Mary Street, now known as Butler's Barracks, speak to an even deeper military history. The earliest dates from 1812, but the complex takes its name from the exploits of Butler's Rangers, the notorious guerrilla fighters who made their winter camp here during the American Revolution. Made up of dispossessed loyalists, disaffected Indigenous Peoples and freed slaves, the Rangers terrorized the American frontier from New York to Virginia. These same grounds were also the headquarters for the British Indian Department, which functioned as the nerve centre for managing diplomatic relations with allied First Nations, as well as wars against the Americans. To Americans of the day, these forces were brutal terrorists, and the pleasant acres of Niagara's Commons were the den of all evil. The barracks remained in military use until the 1960s.

◆ Fort George

Among so much else, Niagara is rich in military history. Fort George was destroyed shortly after its construction 200 years ago, was rebuilt as a Depression-era make-work project and is now designated a National Historic Site. There is programming throughout the summer with costumed re-enactors sharing their musket know-how. The Friends of Fort George also conduct popular nighttime "ghost tours" of the fort. See niagaraghosts.com. Fort George is located at 51 Queen's Parade.

A Matinee at the Shaw Festival

After taking in the town on foot, why not sit down and enjoy a play?

Perhaps even more than the Stratford Festival, the Shaw Festival at Niagara-on-the-Lake is the product of an old-fashioned ensemble that uses familiar actors in any number of roles, Shavian or otherwise. Although the company does mount at least one Shaw play per season, its scope has gradually

Fort George.

The Royal George Theatre on Queen Street hosts a number of Shaw Festival productions each season.

expanded to include all manner of modern plays and musicals. Every year it mounts a dozen productions on several stages, drawing audiences from all over North America to what locals like to call "the prettiest town in Canada."

As with Stratford, the best time to buy tickets to the Shaw Festival plays is well before anyone has seen them, in January or early February, when prices are discounted. That's also when you will have the best choice of dates and seats, especially for the marquee productions, which can sell out quickly. Tickets to weekday performances are the easiest to find, and that's when the town is least likely to be overcrowded.

Shaw also offers a whole roster of events and activities to broaden the experience: seminars, readings, workshops and backstage tours. See shawfest.com for more information and tickets.

As of 2017, the Shaw Festival is operating its own bus service, the **Shaw Express**, which leaves from the Royal York Hotel every morning from Thursday through Sunday, with an afternoon bus on Fridays. The unbeatable price is $25 per person, provided you already have a ticket to a performance. It's the perfect way to see a weekday matinee.

SOUTH

Get outdoors in Lake Erie's Deep South

Let others inch north on overburdened highways as the sunny hours slip by, children squirm and tempers rise. Turn south instead, and you'll be on the beach by the time the crowd clears Barrie. Long overlooked by Torontonians, the north shore of Lake Erie is Canada's deep south, as distinctive in its own way as cottage country to the north. It has its own gestalt, its own accent, a rich cultural history and the last remnants of a Carolinian ecology that is unique in Canada. You can experience the best of it in a tour along the north shore of Long Point Bay, from Port Dover to Backus Woods in Norfolk County. Don't forget to bring a swimsuit.

Swim and Nosh at Port Dover

The starting point is Port Dover, a two-hour drive from Toronto via the QEW, Highway 403 and Highway 6 South. Once a flourishing fishing port and now a somewhat faded resort, apt to be overrun by motorcycles on summer weekends (or any Friday the 13th, when bikers are guaranteed), the town is best known for fish dinners at the Erie Beach Hotel on Walker Street

or Knechtel's down the road — perch or pickerel, fresh caught in the lake. You can also buy fresh fish on the wharf from the Pleasant Port Fish Co., located on Passmore Avenue on the east side of the harbour. If it's not too crowded, swimming and sunning at Port Dover Beach can keep you planted here for the entire day.

Explore Port Ryerse and Normandale

From Dover, head west, following the Waterfront Trail by car or bicycle. You can find a map of the route at waterfronttrail.org. The hamlets of Port Ryerse and Normandale, tucked into wooded ravines where the level plain meets the lake, both date from the 18th century and were bustling places in their day. Now they seem almost magically detached from the wider world, damp and shady in their hollows.

Port Dover Harbour Museum, at 44 Harbour Street, is a definite cut above the usual small-town local history offerings, with a rich collection of artifacts and displays devoted to the maritime history of Lake Erie, the thriving fishery it once supported and the wrecks it has claimed.

Port Dover Beach is a great place to work up an appetite for a fish dinner.

Normandale's tulip tree, the largest in Canada.

RIGHT
The beach at Turkey Point.

The road into Normandale is actually called Spooky Hollow, and if you look up to your left just as it drops down to the shore, you will see Canada's largest tulip tree, a giant of the Carolinian forest and part of the magnolia family, standing proud against the sky.

Exploring Norfolk County by bicycle became easier with the establishment of Ontario's **South Coast Bicycles and Tours** in **Vittoria**. Proprietor John Fulton offers repairs as well as guided tours, and he has a broad range of rentals available, including tandems and e-bikes. See oscbicyclesandtours.com for more information.

Lounge on the Beach at Turkey Point

Turkey Point is another stop that could be a trip in itself, just to lounge on its beach, which is one of the nicest on Lake Erie, surrounded by a cottage community where the simple and sunny 1950s have faded but never quite died. The water here is shallow and warm, making it a favourite destination for local families. There are always dozens of cottages to rent at affordable rates, but facilities for day trippers are scant. The Turkey Point Hotel, at 93 Cedar Drive in Turkey Point, serves reasonable pub grub on a fabulous patio overlooking the beach and the lake.

Bird Watch at Long Point

It's prominent on the map, but the 40-kilometre Lake Erie sand spit

Long Point's wetlands.

known as Long Point is almost unknown to all but north-shore locals. Most of the point has been privately owned for more than a century, preserved for hunting. But when combined with parkland at the top of the spit, the result is an internationally significant wildlife habitat, designated as a UNESCO World Biosphere Reserve due to the importance of its wetlands for migratory waterfowl.

If you're a birder, you know all this. If you're not, Long Point is a terrific place to sample the activity. Established in 1960, the Long Point Bird Observatory is the oldest bird observatory

Before you go, make sure to print off a copy of the **Long Point Birding Trail**, a helpful map and brochure available at birdscanada.org.

OUTDOOR ADVENTURES AT TURKEY POINT

In contrast to the quaint nostalgia of Port Ryerse, Normandale and Turkey Point, **Long Point Eco Adventures** (located, confusingly, at Turkey Point) is pure 21st century and probably the most extensive outdoor-oriented activity centre in the province. It offers some basics like zip-lining, which is the main draw for day trippers, and an extensive network of well-marked mountain bike trails connecting into **Turkey Point Provincial Park**. There are also some very novel alternatives on the menu here, such as stargazing at the park's own observatory and a guided mushroom foray that culminates with a meal made from the day's pickings. See lpfun.ca for more information and bookings.

Backus Woods contains some of Ontario's most established trees.

Hike in Backus Woods

Truth be told, the best possible "eco-adventure" in Norfolk County is a free-of-charge walk in Backus Woods, the largest, most mature Carolinian woodland in Ontario. It's a forest of "inestimable value," according to Ontario Nature, housing some of the oldest trees in the country along with "exceptional numbers of rare and conservative birds and plants." Huge tulip trees, ancient black gums, cucumber trees and sassafras mingle with the usual maple, birch and pine to create an exotic environment, at least by Canadian standards. A well-developed network of trails with signposts and interpretative panels makes it all easily accessible, although fierce bugs and heat can hamper summer visits.

in the Americas, and it now serves as the headquarters of the national organization Bird Studies Canada. You can visit its Old Cut Research Station to see birds being banded, learn about their lives and tour a bird-filled woodlot. It's open to the public during the spring and fall migrations, roughly from April to June and again from August to November.

BIRD BOATING

One of the newest and increasingly popular north-shore excursions carries tourists on fast boats across **Long Point Bay** to the lighthouse at the tip of the spit, the single most remote spot in southern Ontario. Spring birding is the main draw, but **Long Point Tours** (longpointtours.com) and **Long Point Eco Adventures** (lpfun.ca) now conduct daily tours all summer long.

Getting There

The woods are located a few kilometres west of Turkey Point, skirted by Norfolk County Road 24 to the north and Concession Road 3 to the south. There are trailheads with parking off both roads. Alternatively, you can visit the **Backus Heritage Conservation Area**, a pioneer village and campground just to the south of the woods, and hike in from there.

The Niagara Freedom Trail

The Niagara Freedom Trail brings an almost forgotten history — the role of Niagara as a major terminus of the fabled Underground Railroad — vividly to life. It's more a scattering of monuments and plaques than a route per se, but the sum gives a definitively "alt" view of this storied region.

Historians estimate that as many as 40,000 people found freedom on the west bank of the Niagara River, escaping from slavery in the American South and fleeing along the clandestine routes to Canada by "following the North Star." Local towns all supported substantial populations of escaped slaves and their families throughout the 19th century. However, many returned south following the Emancipation Proclamation of 1863, and the story of their lives and struggles dimmed from local memory. The Freedom Trail is an

initiative begun by their descendants, a few dozen families who stayed on for generations in the land where they first found freedom.

St. Catharines: The Salem Chapel

You couldn't get any farther off the well-worn tourist track through the Niagara Peninsula than Geneva Street on the fringe of downtown St. Catharines. And yet, here you will find one of the most significant monuments of black

presence, hemmed in by hectares of emptiness to the east and a used-car lot to the north. The congregation is raising money for emergency repairs to the chapel, though restoration remains a distant dream. When (and if) Tubman's image appears on the U.S. $20 bill, her spiritual home in Canada might also get the attention it deserves.

Niagara-on-the-Lake: Parliament Oak School

It was a U.S. bounty hunter snatching back a freed woman in Niagara and returning her to slavery that inspired Upper Canada's first Governor General, John Graves Simcoe, to write his 1793 *Act Against Slavery*. Simcoe hoped to kill the practice in the cradle of the new colony, but the fact that so many of his colleagues owned slaves themselves forced him to inaugurate the grand tradition of Canadian compromise: keeping the existing slaves in chains while banning the creation of more. It was still the first act of its kind in a British colony. You can find a dignified memorial to the event in the form of a limestone bas-relief on the wall of Parliament Oak School at 325 King Street in Niagara-on-the-Lake, believed to be the site of the colony's first parliament, where the act was passed.

history in Canada, the Salem Chapel of the British Methodist Episcopal (BME) Church, built by former slaves and still a thriving hub for the surviving community of their descendants. This is where legendary Underground Railroad conductor Harriet Tubman worshipped during the 1850s — and planned the daring raids that brought so many more people north to freedom. "I brought them all clear off to Canada," she famously declared, and the first stop was always this neighbourhood of St. Catharines.

The existing 1853 chapel, the third one the congregation built on this site, is the oldest surviving Black church in Ontario. Despite widespread recognition of its importance, it remains a forlorn

Harriet Tubman's Historic Crossing into Canada

In June 2017 the Niagara Parks Commission unveiled a interpretive plaque commemorating Harriet Tubman's first crossing into Canada in 1856, which took place across a suspension bridge near the current Whirlpool Bridge Plaza along the Niagara Parkway north of the falls. Students from nearby schools petitioned for the panel, which details Tubman's life from her time as a slave in Maryland to her escape to freedom in Canada.

Bertie Hall

Thirty kilometres south on the Niagara Parkway brings you to the handsome Bertie Hall, an imposing Greek revival mansion that was used as a warehouse for trade goods in the early 19th century — and also as a safe house where newly escaped slaves could hide while U.S. bounty hunters continued to search for them. A plaque on the grounds details the history of the building and its role in the Underground Railroad. A descent into the basement inside shows where the runaways hid.

The Crossing

The Crossing at Fort Erie marks the spot where thousands of fugitives first set foot in the "Promised Land" of Canada, then a forested shore across from booming Buffalo. Former Maryland slave Josiah Henson, who escaped in 1830 and became a pioneer community builder in Upper Canada, described how "the riotous exultation" of his feelings upon first landing here caused him to fall to the ground and "to execute sundry antics which excited the astonishment of those who were looking on." They thought he was suffering from a seizure. But no, Henson explained, it was his first intoxicating experience of freedom that caused his "fit" of happiness.

You can find a plaque marking the Crossing in the aptly named Freedom Park at the foot of Bertie Street on the Fort Erie waterfront, just across the water from the Land of the Free.

EAST

The industrial sprawl that offends the eye on the eastern approaches to Toronto is deceptive — really no more than a narrow strip of urban ugly enclosed by some of the most picturesque countryside in the province. Nowhere else is the border of Toronto more sharply drawn than on its northeast flank: A bit to the east and a jog north instantly transports you to a world of rolling hills, small farms and old towns that last boomed 150 years ago.

This is also the countryside that has been most completely transformed by mid-century conservation efforts. What was once the "Ganaraska Wasteland" is now the Ganaraska Forest, a busy hive of outdoor recreation. The trail-dense, forested uplands of Glen Major and Walker Woods are growing faster than the suburbs of Whitby, as more and more protected land is added to the complex. Uxbridge now boasts it is the "Trail Capital of Canada." Northumberland County is downright bucolic.

Then there is Prince Edward County, which has lately risen from obscurity to become the leading rural getaway for a new generation of city dwellers.

But as the vogue for "the County" demonstrates, some of these rural retreats are now replete with modern amenities. One needn't travel all the way to the Drake Devonshire in Wellington to discover surprising pockets of sophistication in the hills. Cobourg and Port Hope are both first-class dining and shopping destinations.

The little, lost village of Warkworth in Northumberland is becoming a home decor power centre.

For decades, regional planners and politicians in Durham and beyond complained they didn't get their "fair share" of development. However, that supposed neglect laid the foundations for the area's new identity as a wonderfully preserved anti-Toronto, rich with opportunities for urban escapees.

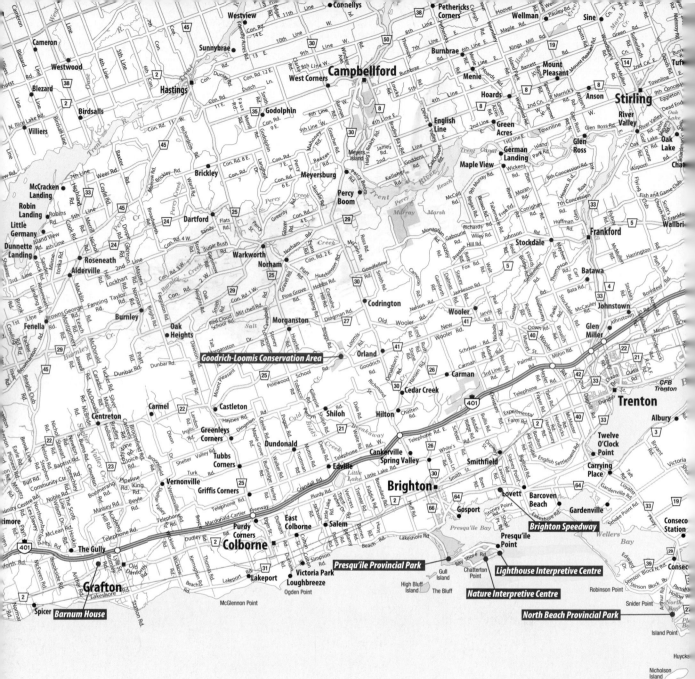

LAKE ONTARIO

EAST

Discover **Oshawa's High Culture**

The McMichael, of course. AGO, check. But those who are truly serious about exploring fine art in southern Ontario will also make time for Oshawa. Yes, Oshawa — ragged flank of the industrial east, working-class, ridiculed and as far off

any beaten tourist track as 70 kilometres could take you.

Robert McLaughlin Gallery

Oshawa's Robert McLaughlin Gallery has long been one of the most active and interesting regional arts centres in

The exterior of the Robert McLaughlin Gallery.

An exhibit inside the Robert McLaughlin Gallery.

the province. Where the McMichael keeps alive the torch of the Group of Seven, the McLaughlin celebrates the iconoclasts who overthrew them, the Painters Eleven group of abstract expressionists, among them Harold Town, Jack Bush and Kazuo Nakamura. The gallery, designed by Hugh Allward and expanded by noted architect Arthur Erickson, has the largest collection of their exuberant canvases in existence, and there are always a dozen on permanent display in their own large space in the gallery.

The collection owes its existence to the advanced taste and generosity of local artist Alexandra Luke, who in 1952 organized the first significant exhibition of abstract art by Canadians — in Oshawa — and went on to convene what became Painters Eleven at her lakefront studio on Thickson Beach (still an intriguing bohemian enclave, hidden behind a wall of factories at the bottom of Thickson Road). As can be seen in the gallery today, Luke's own work is every bit as spectacular as that of the better-known male members of the group. The fledgling Oshawa gallery benefited equally from the patronage of Isabel McLaughlin, daughter of General Motors founder Sam McLaughlin and an accomplished modernist painter in her own right.

In addition to its collection of now-historic abstract art, the gallery

The Painters Eleven were a group of artists who helped introduce abstract expressionism to mainstream Canadian art in the 1950s.

OSHAWA EATS

Contemporary culture needs contemporary food, which is now available in downtown Oshawa. The **Cocoa and Joe Café** offers a gluten-free selection of soups, sandwiches and sweets at 44 Simcoe Street North. The **Berry Hill Food Company** at 82 King Street West serves more ample fare in a clean, modern setting with a shady patio in back.

Some of the pre-1945 Canadian cars found at the Canadian Automotive Museum.

Canadian Automotive Museum

The Canadian Automotive Museum is "cramped, weird and inconvenient," according to the U.S. publication *Hemmings Motor News*, "But visiting is like opening an old shoebox and finding the Hope Diamond inside. It's wonderful."

The wonders include a 1931 Alfa Romeo 6C 1750 Gran Sport Zagato — worth $4-million at auction, "up on bricks behind a pillar," according to *Hemmings* — a large collection of vintage Rolls-Royces and a fascinating array of pre-war oddities from long-forgotten Canadian automakers. Housed in a 1920s Chevrolet-Oakland dealership at 99 Simcoe Street South, the museum is desperately underfunded but steadily upgrading its facilities one infrastructure grant at a time.

also functions as a showcase for the surprising number of accomplished contemporary artists settled in the surrounding hills, where rents are cheap and studios are ample. The extra elbow room of Durham Region seems to have helped produce an abundance of sculptors, among them Ron Baird, Bill Lishman and Victor Tinkl.

The gallery is located at 72 Queen Street, parking is available on site, and admission is free (suggested donation is five dollars). Restaurants are within walking distance.

PARKWOOD NATIONAL HISTORIC SITE

The Robert McLaughlin Gallery is named after the founder of the McLaughlin Carriage Company, who was the father of Sam McLaughlin. Visit **Parkwood**, the estate of Sam McLaughlin and his wife, Adelaide Louise Mowbray, a five-minute drive from the gallery. The art, architecture, furnishings and gardens of the beaux arts–style Parkwood have been faithfully preserved. Guided tours are available. The **Orchid House Tearoom** on site serves tea Tuesday through Sunday from 1:30 p.m. to 4 p.m.

Lose yourself in Glen Major & WALKER WOODS

Let's get lost — but then be back home in time for an early dinner.

There's only one place to go: the sprawling network of conservation lands at the headwaters of Duffins Creek, north of Ajax and south of Uxbridge, which are ideal for hiking, mountain biking, cross-country skiing and snowshoeing.

Like some thriving metropolis of separate but connected forests, this tract goes by many names: The Glen Major Conservation Area connects to Walker Woods, which connects to North Walker Woods in one direction

Fall colours are magnificent in Glen Major Forest.

Navigation posts sprinkled along trails means hikers never get too lost in these woods.

and the Durham Regional Forest in another, the whole forming an irregular patchwork that covers the best part of 50 square kilometres. Within that glorious green sprawl there are hundreds of kilometres of winding trails. Outside Norway, it's my favourite place in the world for cross-country skiing. I'm still finding new routes and views 20 years after discovering this natural wonderland.

From Desert to Forest

Not long ago, there wouldn't have been more than a handful of hard-to-get-at trees still standing on this morainic upland, which ill-advised farming had turned into a scrubby desert of eroded sand hills and dried-up ravines. Such

Be sure to bring a picnic lunch and plenty of water. You could easily spend the whole day here.

were the conditions that inspired the province's original conservationists, and one of the first to see a better future for the devastated landscape was Toronto tax lawyer James Walker.

Beginning in the 1930s with a settler's log cabin from 1854 (which still stands near the western edge of his woods), Walker turned conservation into a business, replanting hundreds of hectares of trees and eventually running a sawmill to reap the harvest. The result was decades of helpful tax losses and an almost-instant woodland, most of which remained untouched when Walker sold his woods for $5 million to the Toronto Region Conservation Authority. This doubled the size of the pre-existing conservation area, and it has continued to grow since.

In many ways, this woodland is bookended by the Albion Hills and conservation areas to the west of Toronto (see pages 16–18), but it is actually larger and much less developed. It's as wild as it gets in the GTA, to the point that there are no facilities of any kind in Glen Major Forest or Walker Woods. There are donation boxes in lieu of admission fees.

Navigating the Wilderness

The only exception to the encompassing wildness is an ingenious system of numbered navigation posts at certain trail intersections, which allows trekkers to pinpoint exactly where they are as they wander. The happy result is that there is no longer any need to carry a map and compass here or, indeed, to follow any sort of planned route through these forests. You're never far from a numbered post with a metal "You Are Here" map affixed to it. Getting lost (briefly) is half the fun.

Terrain and Trails

Each section of the forest has its own character. Trails range from moderate to difficult.

Walker Woods shows its origins as a softwood plantation, though there is a good deal of second-growth hardwood as well. For the most part, its terrain is gently undulating. Anyone wary of skiing or cycling steep, narrow trails should start there.

But if steep and narrow is what you're looking for, Glen Major is the place to be. Its landscape is heavily crumpled, the forest is more varied and a series of slowly regenerating gravel

pits create welcome openings in the woods. This is where you will find the best fall colours and the longest vistas, from the top of the moraine to the distant blue waters of Lake Ontario.

◆ Trans Canada Trail

The Trans Canada Trail traverses a particularly fine stretch of the area, beginning in the Durham Regional Forest to the north and running south through Walker Woods and Glen Major Forest. You can reach it from the northwest corner of Walker Woods on Concession Road 7, at marker

If you are driving Concession Road 7 north of Glen Major on your way to Walker Woods, keep an eye out for the tiny but historic **Glen Major Methodist Church**. The church retains most of its original features, including a pump organ.

Getting There

Three official trailheads serve the main complex of woods. A small parking lot at the corner of Allbright Road and Uxbridge Concession Road 6 (the northern extension of Westney Road) gives access to Walker Woods. A much larger lot, about 4 kilometres south on Concession 6, serves Glen Major. (Watch for the sign announcing East Duffins Headwaters.) There is a third lot at the southeastern corner of the conservation area on Uxbridge Concession 7, just south of the tucked-away village of Glen Major. You can also download a map of the entire system at trca.ca (look up East Duffins Creek Headwaters).

number 8 on the trail map. There is another trailhead at the south end, heading west from where the Uxbridge-Pickering Townline dead ends at Westney Road. The trail zigzags north into Walker Woods.

Annina's Bakeshop

At a time when just about every "four corners" in Ontario can boast of a quaint new café catering to the tourist trade, Annina's Bakeshop still stands out. You need never go anywhere else for butter tarts, but Annina's also serves a broad menu of savoury foods, including some spectacular variations on familiar sandwiches. Located at Highway 47 and Concession Road 3, just northwest of the conservation lands in the village of Goodwood, the shop has become a must-stop destination for all savvy day trippers in the area.

UXBRIDGE

Want to mix a little town with your country? Pay a visit to the town of **Uxbridge**. Start at the **Tin Cup Caffe** on Brock Street for coffee, tea and treats. Afterwards, wander through one of Canada's best independent bookshops, **Blue Heron Books** at 62 Brock. The kids will love a visit to **Parish Lanes**, also on Brock Street, for bowling, arcade games and a classic meal: burger, fries and a soft drink.

SKI RESORTS (WITH AMENITIES)

Three vest-pocket ski resorts in the hills near Glen Major cater to families who prefer more amenities — like groomed trails and heated chalets — than the conservation areas provide. They are actually some of the oldest ski hills in the province, having served as the original out-of-town destinations for the century-old Toronto Ski Club.

Dagmar Ski Resort is the largest, which isn't saying much, but it makes the most of what it has with a substantial terrain park that's especially popular with older children. You can find it at 1220 Lakeridge Road, just east of Glen Major.

Lakeridge and **Skyloft Ski Resorts** are peas in the same pod, both located on Chalk Lake Road just north of Dagmar. Skyloft boasts the highest vertical in the area — over 120 metres — but Lakeridge has more lifts. Both resorts also operate "magic carpet" tows for beginners. They are ideal places to learn to ski or snowboard and much more conveniently located than their rivals farther north.

All three resorts have busy instructional programs and activities for children, and they are small enough that even the youngest kids can play by themselves without leaving your sight. For larger groups, Lakeridge offers obstacle courses, rope-work and climbing at LEEF (Lakeridge Experiential Education Facility).

Cycle Uxbridge Township

There are more bicycles than cars travelling the back roads of Uxbridge Township on any sunny Sunday in the springtime, and the reason is easy to see: Its beautiful, rolling countryside, long-settled and prosperous, makes an especially fine setting for the appearance of the first green things after a long, grey winter. "Rolling" might not quite describe the steady succession of short, steep hills you'll find in this terrain, in the heart of the Oak Ridges Moraine, but that's just one more thing that makes it so attractive to cyclists, especially when the season is new and winter flab needs burning off.

Township Circuits

You can start the day in the pretty town of Uxbridge itself, but the hamlet of Goodwood on Highway 47 is less busy, with parking available at the local community centre. Goodwood is

 Goodwood is famous for more than its butter tarts: It's where CBC's sitcom *Schitt's Creek* is filmed.

The rolling hills of Uxbridge Township.

also the home of Annina's Bakeshop, a first-class bakery-cafe with legendary butter tarts (see page 138). From here you have two basic choices: heading for the "drumlinized uplands" that border the moraine to the north, touring into the heart of the moraine to the east or making a circular route that combines both quadrants. Whatever your route, it's always possible to follow secondary paved roads with light motor traffic.

◆ North to Zephyr and East to Leaskdale

Pedalling 20 kilometres north of Goodwood along Concession Road 3 brings you to the crossroads of Zephyr. Along the way, you can stop by Cooper's, a CSA farm and maze, located at 266 Ashworth Road. Ride east on Zephyr Road and then south on Concession Road 7 (10 kilometres), and you will find Leaskdale, a hideaway village that looks like it could have been ripped from the pages of *Anne of Green Gables* — and was indeed the home of *Green Gables* author Lucy Maud Montgomery for most of her literary life. During the summer season, the Lucy Maud Montgomery Society of Ontario operates a tea and gift shop in the yellow-brick church next to the manse where Montgomery lived with her clergyman husband and children. The manse, which is open daily for tours in the summer months, is a National Historic Site.

Five kilometres south of Leaskdale on Concession Road 7 brings you to the Thomas Foster Memorial, surely one of

the most outlandish — and beautiful — architectural follies in Canada. Built as a personal mausoleum by a successful Toronto businessman in 1935, it is a cut-down Taj Mahal rendered in a Byzantine style, with a spectacular interior of marble and stained glass that is often used for concerts. Tours are available most days during the summer. See fostermemorial.com for more information. It's another 20 kilometres back south and west to Goodwood.

Both circuits are long and challenging, so you'll definitely want a butter tart from Annina's by the time you finish. Pack plenty of snacks and water for the ride.

◆ East over the Moraine

The roads east of Goodwood and south of Uxbridge cross some of the least developed, most heavily wooded terrain of the Oak Ridges Moraine. The best route is to follow Regional Road 21 (Goodwood Road) east of Goodwood to Concession Road 6 (Westney Road), and then ride 10 kilometres south on Westney, past Walker Woods and Glen Major (see pages 135–8) to Pickering Concession Road 8. Two kilometres east is the intersection of Sideline 4. Turn left onto Sideline 4 and the route takes you back north over the moraine and into the ski hills for 10 kilometres. Turn east (right) onto Chalk Lake Road and then north (left) onto Ashburn Road, 3 kilometres later. Follow Ashburn and Mast Roads back

The Byzantine style Thomas Foster Memorial.

LEFT
A statue of Lucy Maud Montgomery in Leaskdale.

The restored trestle bridge is a treat for cyclists and hikers looking to explore Uxbridge.

to Regional Road 21, and then ride 12 kilometres back west to Goodwood.

The Uxbridge Trestle Bridge and Barton Trail Route

If you are travelling with children and would prefer a shorter, less hilly trail, a short rail trail starts at the York Durham Heritage Railway on Railway Street in Uxbridge. The station, also known as Witch's Hat (see it to find out why!), is home to a small railway museum. The trail itself crosses a heritage wooden trestle bridge built in 1872 by the Toronto-Nipissing Railway and restored in 2015. You can continue for another 2 kilometres along the Barton Trail, which passes through fields, woods and a pond. There is also a playground and picnic area on the way. Visit discoveruxbridge.ca/trails for a map of the Barton Trail Route and many more.

"TRAIL CAPITAL OF CANADA"

Uxbridge Township's 220 kilometres of beautiful trails run through historic villages, forests, wetlands and meadows, and they include opportunities for hiking, skiing, snowshoeing, mountain biking and even horseback riding. For a searchable list of trails, visit discoveruxbridge.ca/trails.

Winter in Lake Scugog

You can find some of the best cross-country ski terrain anywhere outside Norway on the Oak Ridges Moraine and the Niagara Escarpment, which are Toronto's natural borderlands. What you can't find so easily anymore is the snow that makes the sport possible. However, the freeze-thaw cycles that have replaced the old snowy winters have created an interesting effect: For much of the winter, local lakes and ponds are glassy smooth. Freezing rain in January is nature's own Zamboni, and the result is far more winter days amenable to long,

free skates on natural ice. Suddenly, "Nordic skating" is a thing.

Skating the Lake Scugog Shoreline

The best place to try Nordic skating near Toronto is Lake Scugog. It's big and has lots of natural shoreline to

Lake Scugog is an artificial lake that was created when a local settler dammed the Scugog River to power his grist mill in 1834.

Lake Scugog's conditions make its shores ideal for ice fishing and skating.

explore, has little or no current and is so shallow it can be more ice than water by mid-February. It's graced with the ideal staging point for a winter expedition: the cozy little town of Port Perry. It's also where you'll find fishing huts from shore to shore. These people know their ice.

Conditions permitting, the most interesting area to explore is the extensive marshland south of the Highway 7A bridge, where an old-money Toronto family maintains an enormous duck-hunting preserve that is 3 kilometres deep and as many wide. Heading north, you can skirt Scugog Island, home to the Mississaugas of Scugog Island First Nation, or you can veer west and skate up the flat and meandering Nonquon River.

STAYING SAFE ON THE ICE

The new universal mantra among public authorities in Ontario is "No ice is safe ice." This can be true even if you're skating on a hard-frozen lake dotted with fishing huts. Ice is always treacherous over even slightly moving water, and conditions can change by the hour. At a minimum, you should carry a set of ice claws, which allow you to drag yourself back up onto the ice should you fall through, and at least one sharp pole to test the ice's thickness as you go. The claws, which you wear on a lanyard around your neck, are available for a few dollars at Canadian Tire. Ski or walking poles fitted with sharp metal picks help push you along as well as keep you safe. And because you are as likely to be an observer as a victim of an accident, it's a good idea to carry a rescue throw bag of the sort all small boats in Canada are required to have on board.

Ice Fishing on the Lake

If skating the icy acres isn't winter enough for you — or you'd prefer someone else to do the hard parts — you might be interested in an ice-fishing adventure. In any given winter, there could be hundreds of fishing huts out on the ice here. Either Scugog Ice Adventures (scugogiceadventures.com) or Lake Scugog Ice Hut Rentals (lakescugogicehutrentals.com) will set you up with everything you need for a full day or an afternoon.

The **Lake Scugog Pond Hockey Charity Tournament** is played on a Saturday every February at the Port Perry marina. Come for the day!

Prefer your fish on a plate? **Captain George Fish and Chips** at 161 Queen Street, a stone's throw from the Port Perry marina, has firm, fresh and crispy halibut among other dishes. The **Piano Café** is another popular dining spot on Queen Street.

Ice huts are available for rental for those looking to try ice fishing.

Historic Downtown Port Perry

The charm of Port Perry is its handsome main drag, Queen Street, with its beautifully preserved Victorian architecture and fine collection of bistros, bakeries and taverns a stone's throw from the town dock. It sweeps directly down to the shore of Lake Scugog, creating a continuous red-brick frame for the sparkling waters and the farms

Queen Street in Port Perry.

beyond. It's rare for an upland Ontario town to communicate so respectfully with its own landscape, and Port Perry makes the most of its special character, having become a favourite destination for shoppers and browsers throughout the region. The historic downtown is crowded with as many fashion boutiques as you will find in a mall, and just as many shops selling country decor and gifts, like Luke's Country Store at 207 Queen and Meta4 Gallery nearby. But there's not a single mall-like chain store among them.

 Willow Books is a hidden treasure of used and rare books located in a small alley behind Captain George Fish and Chips.

SUMMERTIME IN PORT PERRY

Port Perry is also a summer destination, with lots of boating and fishing opportunities. Hike the north end of **Scugog Island** and its ecologically significant wetland. The **Port Perry Marina**'s waterfront patio serves breakfast, lunch and dinner.

Race to Canadian Tire

MOTORSPORT PARK

It has been decades since Mosport Park (now the Canadian Tire Motorsport Park) regularly broke national sports attendance records with the wheel-to-wheel action of Canadian racing's Golden Age. It culminated in the wild excess of the Can-Am series, which saw the most powerful sports cars ever built thunder through the green hills north of Oshawa. These days, it's racing itself that makes the trek, staging its premier events on cramped and ugly street courses in the cities. But Mosport is the opposite of that: a classic 4-kilometre, 10-turn loop through rolling terrain that, unlike many other circuits of its kind and era, remains remarkably untamed today.

These days, there are only a few ticketed events available to the general public each season. Most fans come for the weekend and camp on site, another great holdover from Mosport's heyday. Sunday-only tickets are cheap and promise the best action. You'll be surprised to find how much fun it can be to watch motor racing in its natural environment.

The scenic view from the sidelines at Canadian Tire Motorsport Park.

Facilities

In addition to the road course and paddock, where you can view the cars up close, the park offers hectares of parkland and open fields to explore, including walking and mountain biking trails. Washrooms are available throughout the park.

Activities at the paddock include games for kids, high-tech simulators and other interactive experiences, depending on the event.

Bring along your own picnic or eat at Pinty's Trackside Grill. Concession stands also offer snacks and meals on event days.

Events

Here are some of the highlights among the park's ticketed events:

• The season begins with Victoria Day weekend's Speedfest, a varied program of stock car racing currently headlined by the Canadian-only NASCAR Pinty's Series.

• For many, the true highlight comes every June when the Vintage Auto Racing Association of Canada stages its annual Canadian Historic Grand Prix. Simply seeing such an exotic collection of often museum-quality machines is one thing; watching them flogged mercilessly in hard-fought races through the bends of a legendary circuit is something else entirely.

• The biggest event of the year is currently the Mobil 1 SportsCar Grand

FAMILY FUN

Admission is free for kids 16 and under and the whole park is family friendly. Camping in the rough is also available if you want to enjoy a longer family weekend.

Prix in early July, highlighted by the only Canadian race of the IMSA WeatherTech SportsCar Championship series, which features exotic prototype and GT race cars.

Mosport ain't what it used to be, but then again, it is.

Beyond the Races
◆ Tyrone Mills

Need a bit of a quiet country break after your day at the races? Busy Durhamites with grain to grind, lumber to plane and a yen for apple cider doughnuts have long enjoyed the benefit of one-stop shopping at Tyrone Mills, located on Concession Road 7, a few kilometres southwest of Mosport. No mere museum, the mill has been putting the power of Bowmanville Creek to commercial use continuously since 1846. Although most of its income now comes from sales of baked goods, the mill still mills grain and dresses lumber using technology that hasn't changed for more than 170 years. The fall of the creek from an earthen dam spins an underwater turbine connected directly to a massive millstone in the centre of the store, with belts and pulleys transferring the power upstairs to a museum-quality collection of vintage woodworking tools. It's an amazing showpiece of industrial archaeology, even more so when you consider that

young Sam McLaughlin, the General Motors founder who grew up on a nearby farm, would have been a regular customer more than a century ago.

Mill owner Robert Shafer takes on a variety of custom work, but he has become an expert in matching the mouldings of baseboards and other wood trim for historical house restorations. All that and doughnuts, too.

Tyrone Mills is a fascinating side trip away from the roaring engines.

ABOVE
Canadian Tire Motorsport Park offers on-site camping.

Cattle grazing in the Greenbelt.

RIGHT
Gallery on the Farm near Enniskillen.

The mill, located at 2656 Concession Road 7 in Tyrone, is open to visitors most days, except when there's a big milling job to be done. Call 905-263-8871 to make sure. If you're lucky, you'll be able to persuade owner Shafer to conduct a full tour, including the usually off-limits woodworking shop.

◆ Farms in the Greenbelt

When the Friends of the Greenbelt Foundation need a success story to tell — one that epitomizes the best of what the Ontario Greenbelt is meant to achieve — they often point to 1721 Regional Road 3 in Durham (just west of the hilltop hamlet of Enniskillen), the picture-perfect farm where Eric and Jenny Bowman raise and sell organic beef. The Bowmans also operate a small gallery and gift shop, hence Gallery on the Farm. Their signature product, sold frozen, is terrific.

If you're inquisitive, you'll also learn a lot about the challenges and rewards of organic farming in the GTA. They suggest you contact them ahead of time as the property is an active farm. Email galleryonthefarm@hotmail.com or call 905-263-8245.

Another innovative agricultural operation worth a short detour is Geissberger Farmhouse Cider at 5345 Langmaid Road, which has been pressing local apples into delicious sweet cider since 1970. The innovation is Geissberger's "bag-in-box" packaging, which keeps the untreated drink fresh for up to three months. The Geissberger family also operates the only mobile apple press east of the Rockies, travelling from farm to farm turning excess apples that might otherwise rot on the ground into a long-lasting elixir. If you want to visit their farm store, call 905-728-8674 and let them know when you'd like to stop by.

Get outdoors in the Ganaraska Forest

Just an hour east of Toronto lies a year-round outdoor paradise — a forest brimming with recreational opportunities, covering 4,452 hectares of the area from the eastern edge of Clarington municipality to mid-Northumberland County and north of County Road 9 to south of Highway 115.

From Wasteland to Wonderland: The Ganaraska Forest

In the postwar years, this broad upland tract was known as the Ganaraska Wasteland, a devastated barren of sand hills and dry gullies that spilled flash floods downstream with every heavy rainfall. Today it is the largest contiguous forest in southern Ontario.

The transformation of the Ganaraska River watershed was the original signature project of a mid-century conservation movement, which was triggered by the almost total deforestation of the southern province. Its tremendous success inspired the creation of 35 other regional conservation authorities, divided by watersheds rather than political boundaries, which together have

The Ganaraska
Forest Centre.

already committed to horseback riding, mountain biking, skiing, snowmobiling, hunting, tree climbing or ATVing, you probably know this forest. If you're interested in trying any of the above, it's all here.

♦ Ganaraska Forest Centre

The centre of the action is the Ganaraska Forest Centre (GFC), which has grown from a lone Quonset hut into a busy multi-use outdoor education facility. Several well-marked hiking and ski trails loop out from here at a trailhead. Day passes or annual memberships are required to use them. The GFC has washroom facilities and a picnic area near the parking lot. There is also a changing area, and a canteen adjacent to the centre that operates on weekends from the beginning of May through to the end of October.

managed an environmental turn-around as dramatic as the pillage that first created the wastes. From this base, and with the help of much subsequent legislation, a great arc of forestland has grown, almost completely encircling the GTA sprawl.

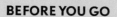

And what fun it is. As the first and still largest forest of its kind, the Ganaraska has grown into a hotbed of outdoor enthusiasms, just as intended by the far-sighted conservationists of the 1940s. If you're

♦ Climbing and Zipping

A few hundred metres into the forest you will encounter the fabulous rigging of the Treetop Trekking Ganaraska adventure park, with zip lines, high catwalks, rope ladders and swings

BEFORE YOU GO

There are a few things to note before you make the journey:

- Poison ivy is abundant throughout the Ganaraska Forest, so be sure to wear long pants or tights, socks and shoes before venturing out.
- Trails are well marked, but take a forest trail map (available at ganaraskaforestcentre.ca) with you. Cyclists should also bring a compass and a GPS with them.
- Be aware that hunting is permitted, especially in the east and west forest areas. Consult the forest map.
- Dogs are permitted in the forest, but they must be on leash in the central section.

lacing the tall pines high overhead. This is one of six such parks in Ontario offered by the Quebec-based company, and it promises the province's "most extreme aerial course" along with easier climbs for beginners. Be sure to phone 1-855-280-0900 or email ganaraska@treetoptrekking.com to reserve a guided tour.

• Horseback Riding

Horseback riding has long been a fixture of the Ganaraska, with several nearby clubs and facilities giving riders access to its hundreds of kilometres of trails. Trail rides for the horseless are available on weekends at Maple Crescent Farm, located at 9741 County Road 10. To get there, follow Ganaraska Road 8 kilometres east from Cold Springs Road and then north 4 kilometres on County Road 10. Phone 905-797-2598 to book rides. Another option is Trickle Creek Farms, located on the 10th Line of Millbrook, just north and east of Maple Crescent. To book rides, phone 705-872-8286.

• Hiking and Cycling

If hiking is your thing, the forest's hiking trails traverse mixed forest and rolling hills, where you can spot deer, wild turkeys, songbirds and birds of prey.

ABOVE
Visitors can enjoy ziplining and climbing in the Ganaraska Forest.

Inviting trails await winter hikers, snowshoers and cross-country skiers.

The serene fields of Laveanne Lavendar Farm.

out of the main trail, or even just to follow your nose through the maze. In any case, you definitely need to carry a compass and GPS if you venture into these woods without a guide.

◆ Skiing and Snowshoeing

More than 30 kilometres of groomed ski trails, along with another 10 for snowshoers, fan out from the Ganaraska Forest Centre on Cold Springs Camp Road. Unlike the cycling trails, these are fairly easy and suitable for novices. You can rent both cross-country and snowshoeing equipment through the GFC as well.

Exploring the Ganaraska Valley

◆ The Village of Orono

Billing itself with justification as "a lively little village," nearby Orono, southwest of the Ganaraska Forest, offers respite from the exertions of outdoor exercise with a handful of restaurants and antique stores in a picturesque setting. Try the Orono Country Café or the licensed Fire Hall Bistro. Both are located on Main Street.

Held the first weekend after Labour Day, the annual Orono Fair is one of the oldest in the province and a model of its type, with lots of rides, concerts, tractor pulls and prize veggies.

The Ganaraska is also a mountain biking hotbed, with hundreds of kilometres of single- and double-track trails flowing through a completely naturalized, roadless setting. The classic single-track route through the central forest, called the EPIC Trail, is one of only four Canadian routes — and the only one east of British Columbia — to be designated "EPIC" by the International Mountain Biking Association for providing "a true backcountry riding experience that is technically and physically challenging."

The 60-kilometre route is permanently marked, with black arrows on pink signs, and sticks to single-track in the central forest, which is off limits to motorbikes and ATVs. There are plenty of opportunities to cut shorter loops

• Laveanne Lavender Farm

One of the prettiest attractions in the Ganaraska Valley appears every July when the blossoms open and a purple haze envelops Laveanne. A pioneering lavender farm that aims to create a touch of Provence in the Northumberland hills, the farm currently tends 10,000 plants growing over 1.5 hectares, as well as a lavender maze for meditation, a program of lavender-centred seminars and a gift shop selling bodycare products handmade on the farm. At the height of the bloom, you can participate in lavender yoga and eat a lavender-infused lunch at the farm's pop-up restaurant. The farm is located at 8667 Gilmour Road, just north of the hamlet of Campbellcroft.

• Linwood Acres Trout Farm

Why not pick up some fish while in the neighbourhood? Linwood Acres Trout Farm is located just south of Laveanne on Gilmour Road. You can buy fresh or smoked trout here, or you can catch your own in one of the farm's spring-fed ponds. Ice fishing in the winter is also available.

Camp 30

Camp 30, a former POW camp for high-ranking Nazi prisoners during World War II located near Bowmanville, is a lesser-known but intriguing piece of Canadian history.

The bad news about Camp 30 is that visitors are no longer able to poke around the site, enter the abandoned buildings or fantasize freely about its eventful past, as they once were.

The good news is that the vandals and arsonists who did so much damage to the site in years past are likewise barred while Camp 30 undergoes a long-delayed restoration. By the end of the work, the camp's surviving buildings will become the site of a municipal park integrated into a new housing development, Bowmanville's answer to Toronto's Distillery District and Evergreen Brickworks, according to local officials. It's a fascinating place with a rich and unique history, and one that could easily emerge from its makeover as a popular attraction. In the meantime, visitors are instructed to stay on the outside, looking in.

You can find Camp 30 at 2226 Lambs Road, which runs north of Highway 2, just east of the town of Bowmanville.

Interested in finding out more about Camp 30 before you visit? If you have school-age kids, they might enjoy Eric Walter's Camp X series of novels, which tell the story of two brothers who delivered mail to the top-secret camp during World War II.

EAST

Tour Port Hope

There is often a fatal point at which naturally attractive places become intolerably touristy, but Port Hope balances gracefully on the edge. It's a lovely historic town where hardware stores still outnumber fudge shops, antiquing is still rewarding and the pleasure of discovery is easily obtained. Visiting Port Hope is also one of the few genuine small-town excursions that can still be done entirely by rail, without the need for a car.

What keeps Port Hope "authentic" for excursionists today is the town's bad luck. The early operation of the historic Eldorado uranium refinery, whose contemporary descendant still dominates the local waterfront, scattered low-level nuclear waste throughout the town and surrounding countryside. The painstaking cleanup has long dominated Port Hope's public life and, until completed, forestalls the future one might expect for a place so favoured. In the meantime, the town remains wonderfully characteristic of old Ontario — but with much better food.

Historic Lakeshore Road: A Scenic Entrance

One of the pleasures of Port Hope is the ability to drive there on a road as old and pretty as the town itself. To find it, leave Highway 401 East at Newtonville Road (Exit 448) and drive south to Lakeshore Road. (If you exit 14 kilometres earlier at Newcastle, you can enjoy a small beach near the Newcastle Marina before continuing on your way.) Heading east on Lakeshore, you will pass through an undisturbed museum of 19th-century Canadiana, including the hamlet of Wesleyville, formerly a ghost town that is being brought back to life with the restored Wesleyville United Church as its hub. In addition to the church, an abandoned century home, a schoolhouse and the cemetery remain. Visit wesleyvillevillage.com for more about the hamlet's history. Slip past the ghost town of Port Britain and into Port Hope.

Commercial Walton Street

Port Hope's modestly famous main street is not only one of the best-preserved examples of the type in the province, it has the most character. Rather than tracing a grid line on the plain, it drops irregularly down the bank of the Ganaraska River toward the shore of Lake Ontario, lined on both sides by handsome commercial buildings that confidently embrace a boom town future that never arrived.

The Ganaraska River flows through Port Hope.

LEFT
The restored Wesleyville United Church.

A view of Walton Street from Queen Street.

One of Ontario's best selections of antique and decor shops adds to the pleasure of simply being there. The shopping extends up and down Walton on both sides, south along John Street and north on Ontario.

Here you will also discover a healthy assortment of modern restaurants and cafés. Walking a little farther south along the riverside, toward the impressive 1850 railway viaduct that spans the valley, brings you to Olympus Burgers, a favourite among both locals and tourists. Farther south still, Crawford's Lakeside Café, at 125 Mill Street South, offers waterfront views.

Bibliophiles will not want to miss **Furby House Books** at 65 Walton Street. Audiophiles should head to the **Northumberland Rock and Roll Experience** at No. 27 for some unique musical artifacts.

Heritage Walking Tour

Heritage is serious business in Port Hope, which prides itself on having more than 200 buildings designated under the Ontario Heritage Act, more than any other town in Canada per capita. It's easy to take a self-guided walking tour. Check out these highlights:

• See two elegant examples of the early "Yankee" style of Ontario architecture.

The 1834 Bluestone House is located on picturesque Dorset Street East (No. 21), and the 1800 Elias Smith House at 168 King is the oldest house in Port Hope and reputed to be the setting for Jane Urquhart's celebrated novel *Away*.

- St. Mark's Anglican Church, which is located in the same neighbourhood at 51 King Street, dates from 1822.
- St. Lawrence Hall Block at 87 Walton Street is a four-storey Italianate design circa 1853.
- Gillett Paterson Block at 29–33 Walton Street is an early (1845) commercial building with Greek revival elements.
- The Town Hall and its elegant cupola are located at 56 Queen Street.

For a more intensive experience, the local branch of the Architectural Conservancy of Ontario has published photographs and histories of every listed structure. This inventory, titled *Symbols of Our Past,* is available for purchase at Furby House Books, while supplies last. Visit acoporthope.ca for more information about tours and the branch's ongoing projects.

The local visitor's bureau, at 20 Queen Street, distributes maps for self-guided walking tours. Beyond that, the bureau is an excellent source of information about all things Port Hope.

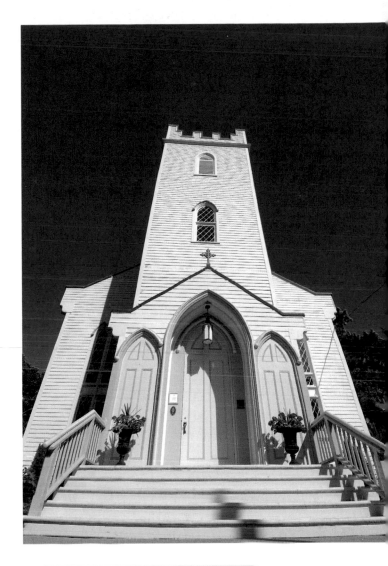

St. Mark's Anglican Church is one of the historical highlights of Port Hope.

The ACO's annual **Port Hope House Tour**, held every fall for more than half a century, offers a view inside some of the town's notable homes. It sells out quickly, so advance planning is necessary.

The Capitol Theatre's distinctive sign.

remaining "atmospheric" theatres, with an interior designed to resemble an open-air medieval courtyard surrounded by trees, all lovingly restored to its original glory.

Although you are more likely to find Disney than Shakespeare on the bill at the Capitol, visiting it can be an attractive alternative to the Shaw or Stratford Festivals. There are matinees throughout the season, making it easy to schedule theatre-and-dining day trips, with or without train connections. See capitoltheatre.com for schedules and tickets.

Exploring the Outskirts

A short drive from downtown will bring you to some fun and offbeat attractions.

◆ Primitive Designs

Located just north of Port Hope on County Road 28, Primitive Designs offers one of the strangest, most enjoyable retail experiences you will ever encounter. It's a mad smorgasbord of handicrafts, furniture and decor, imported mainly from Southeast Asia and crammed into a 740-square-metre shed, with more spilling over the grounds. Whether you need a sheet-metal donkey barbecue, a thatched-roof Timorese pagoda, a slab of exotic wood or a lizard sculpture,

Shows at the "Atmospheric" Capitol Theatre

One architectural experience not to be missed in Port Hope is a visit to the historic Capitol Theatre on Queen Street, a grand 1930s movie palace that now hosts a professional theatre company that stages plays and musicals year round, along with concerts, films and any number of community events. The Capitol is one of the country's last

this is the place to go. Presiding over all is a collection of the most remarkable scrap-metal sculptures, including a life-size T-Rex and a whole family of giant robots, the largest standing 7 metres. The place is completely crazy and wildly popular.

♦ Haute Goat

The most recent entry in Port Hope's eccentric-attraction sweepstakes is Haute Goat, an award-winning rural theme park devoted to all things caprid. Owners Shain Jaffe and Debbie Nightingale let their imaginations run free on the farm, located on a high hill overlooking the Ganaraska Valley. Here you can participate in what they call a "shmurgle" — a session of hugging baby goats and alpacas. Or you can enjoy the uplifting experience of goat yoga. And, of course, there is a gift shop selling every manner of goat produce, from milk and cheese to cheesy souvenirs.

To find the farm from Port Hope, travel west on Highway 2 to County Road 65, then north 4 kilometres to the intersection of the 5th Line. Haute Goat is located about 1 kilometre west of the intersection.

Some locals at Haute Goat.

ABOVE
Scrap-metal robots guard the grounds of Primitive Designs.

Midway between Port Hope and Cobourg, along County Road 2, you'll find **Betty's Pies and Tarts** in a roadside house at No. 7380. You might miss it, but if you do, turn around! Betty's has some award-winning butter tarts and an amazing array of fruit tarts and pies, all at great prices.

EAST

Splash around Cobourg

Cobourg is in many ways the lakeside twin to Port Hope, just 10 kilometres west, sharing the same history of quick ascent followed by a long decline and fitful 20th-century gentrification. Although it is less charismatic than its twin, Cobourg has one summer attraction that easily justifies a trip to its shores: one of the finest beaches on the north shore of Lake Ontario.

Sun and Sand

Long before tourists began trekking east to Prince Edward County for its pristine sand beaches, this waterfront was the playground of wealthy Americans in search of pure air and clean water. Careful stewardship has kept it that way, and Cobourg Beach is still as pretty as can be: a long, wide crescent backing onto a shady park, with the

Quaint **Harbourlight Delights** on Division Street just north of the beach has a great selection of soft and hard ice cream to enjoy after a hot day in the sun.

added advantage of a historic town to explore just a block away.

The beach itself is large and clean, the water shallow enough in places for kids to play in and adults to wade in. There's also a splash pad and play structures close by. You don't have to venture far for amenities: there are washrooms and change rooms on site, as well as a concession stand where you can get ice cream. Please note dogs are not allowed on the beach. Kayaks, canoes and paddleboards are available for rent at Green Canoe Outfitters at the east end of the beach near Breakers Motel.

At the west end of the beach, you can walk out to the East Pierhead Lighthouse and the marina is next door. You can also take a break from the beach in nearby Victoria Park, where they have shaded picnic tables.

The Cobourg West Beach, west of the marina, is a mix of pebbles and sand. It also has a naturalized grass area, a boardwalk and an Ecology Garden, which is maintained by locals. West Beach is a quiet alternative to the busy main beach.

Victoria Hall and the Historic Town

Foremost among Cobourg's many early buildings is Victoria Hall, an extraordinary high Victorian folly that has dominated King Street since 1860. Built in a neoclassic style similar to that of Toronto's St. Lawrence Hall, this small-town version is actually larger and more opulent than its urban

Victoria Hall on King Street.

LEFT
A lifeguard keeps a watchful eye over Cobourg's lovely sandy beach.

equivalent. Bumptious little Cobourg went broke building it and then went to sleep for a century. The interior is less impressive, but climbing to the attic will bring you to the Art Gallery of Northumberland.

Most of the shops and restaurants in Cobourg are located within a few blocks of Victoria Hall. If you care to explore, the Cobourg Tourism Centre at 212 King Street West distributes a brochure outlining walking tours of the historic town.

On Two Wheels: Cycling around Cobourg

Apart from its own charms, Cobourg is ideally situated as a jumping-off point for some of the loveliest cycling tours in southern Ontario.

The big draw is Northumberland County's wonderful rolling topography and its crooked roads with very light traffic. You can drive another hour east to reach the popular cycling routes of Prince Edward County — and thousands do — but to get there you will bypass some of the best cycling terrain in the province.

Local cycling clubs have established dozens of different routes of varied length and difficulty, but some of the best of them are officially designated and marked with roadside signs. There is also a wealth of detailed information about cycling in the county available online at northumberlandtourism.com and ontariobybike.ca.

◆ Rice Lake and Shelter Valley Cycling Routes

There are two noteworthy cycling routes for the more adventurous. The 74-kilometre Rice Lake Ramble is the emergent classic of Northumberland

cycling tours, shirking no hills as it circles the heart of the county. You'll need a fair degree of fitness and a full day to complete it comfortably. But you'll never be sorry you tried. The hills are especially magnificent in the fall.

The route heads north out of Cobourg to the scenic south shore of Rice Lake, east to the Alderville First Nation and then south past Peter's Woods (see pages 167–8) back to Cobourg.

The 50-kilometre Shelter Valley Cycling Route is no less hilly yet less daunting for casual cyclists. You can cut it even shorter and avoid traffic along County Road 2 by beginning the ride 7 kilometres east of Cobourg at the corner of No. 2 and Brookside Road. The route offers "a little bit of everything in a beautiful bundle of hills, vistas of Lake Ontario, old century barns, long fast flats, tree canopies and the lovely Shelter Valley Creek," according to Ganaraska Freewheelers President Jen Poole.

You can find maps for both of these routes at northumberlandtourism.com.

On the challenging Rice Lake Ramble, cyclists sample the best of Northumberland County.

EAST

Drive the Northumberland County Circuit

To modern Torontonians, the pleasure of a country drive must seem as antique as the warm glow of a kerosene lantern. Even after breaking through the surrounding sprawl, the pleasure-seeking motorist is faced with endless kilometres of gridded roads with nary a bend or a swoop in sight. But the effort of escape is rewarded when the trip begins with a beeline east to Northumberland County.

You'd be hard pressed to find a straight road or a dull view in this age-lessly rustic landscape. Locals will affirm that the cattle of Northumberland are born with legs longer on one side than the other so they can stand straight in the hills. It's also where you'll find one of the last tracts both of old-growth forest and black-oak savannah in the province. Although much less known and visited than more-distant Prince Edward County, it is far more scenic.

The Loop

Traffic is scarce, villages are quaint, stoplights and strip malls are non-existent. This driving route is less than 90 kilometres long but could easily take all day, with time allowed for

hikes in two conservation areas and lunch in Warkworth, a hideaway village now home to a substantial gay community.

◆ Grafton to Peter's Woods

The loop begins in the village of Grafton, just east of Cobourg at Exit 487 of Highway 401. Before heading north, take time to travel a few kilometres west of Grafton on Highway 2 to visit Barnum House, a very fine example of Yankee-style Greek revival architecture, built in 1819 by a Loyalist from Vermont. Although restored and converted into a museum, it is now sadly closed to the public.

Travelling north from Grafton on Lyle Street (County Road 23) brings you to the picturesque four-corners community of Centreton. On the way, you can detour to the west on Academy Hill Road to visit Ste. Anne's Bakery. The bakery prepares gluten-free baked goods using ingredients grown on the property of Ste. Anne's Spa, which is located around the corner on Massey Road.

Continuing on County Road 23, keep travelling north past Centreton on the same road (renamed McDonald) and follow the twists and turns for 5 kilometres until you come to the sign, on the east side of the road, for Peter's Woods.

The size of the trees you will encounter here in this vest-pocket wilderness is inversely proportional to the size of the land they now occupy: What was once a magnificent climax forest and savannah blanketing all of southern Ontario can now be encompassed in a circular trail less than 1 kilometre in length. Avid foresters will point out other patches of old-growth elsewhere

Young explorers discover the wonders of Peter's Woods.

LEFT
Barnum House, near Grafton, is a worthy detour for those interested in Yankee-style architecture.

Cute cafés, galleries and boutiques line Warkworth's Main Street.

◆ Lunch Break in Warkworth

Fifty years ago it was Niagara-on-the-Lake. Thirty years ago it was Elora. Today, it's Prince Edward County. But deep in the hills of Northumberland County there is Warkworth, another slumbering beauty brought back to life thanks to the enthusiasm of both its long-time residents and its new ex-urban gentry.

As thoroughly hidden away as any surviving village in the province, little Warkworth stands out because of its inclusivity and strong gay community. The result is a lively arts scene and a surprisingly sophisticated collection of boutiques, galleries and cafés lining Main Street. With stores like the Cheeky Bee, The General, 13 and 1, metaphorhome and Winker's Nook, Warkworth has become a virtual power centre in the country home furnishing segment.

The food scene is less developed, but the recent opening of the farm-to-table restaurant 'Sper was much acclaimed by local trendsetters. For snacks, the savoury and sweet buns at the Bakery are first-rate. Visit with your kids in mid-March for the old-time Maple Syrup Festival, complete with wagon rides. Go to warkworth.ca for more information about the town and local events, such as Art in the Park, the annual Lilac Festival and the Long Lunch, to name a few.

in the province, but they are no more than that.

But as patches go, Peter's Wood is first rate. Most impressive are the immense white pines that rise straight and branchless for 20 metres or more before reaching the sun.

A nice touch here is the availability of an interpretive guide to the forest from an unmanned kiosk at the trailhead. The trail itself is well maintained and can be completed in less than half an hour – a perfect warm-up for lunch and shopping in the village of Warkworth.

To get to Warkworth, continue north on McDonald Road past Peter's Wood and turn right (east) onto County Road 29. It's about 18 kilometres down County Road 29.

◆ Warkworth to Rice Lake Plains

The next stage of the loop leads to the Goodrich-Loomis Conservation Area, another low-profile ecological landmark. To get there from Warkworth, travel south on County Road. 25, through the hamlet of Morganston, and turn left onto Huycke Road. Turn left again at the T-intersection and drive another 4 kilometres on the Pinewood School Road.

This sparsely visited conservation area epitomizes the charm of the local scenery. It also preserves another ecological treasure: the last remnants of the Rice Lake Plains, once a 125-kilometre long band of open prairie and black-oak savannah. Several trails leading from the conservation centre give access both to the grasslands and the banks of Cold Creek, one of the finest trout streams in eastern Ontario.

To complete the loop, backtrack west on Pinewood School Road, past Huycke, turn left (south) onto Tobacco Road, and then right (west) onto Dingman Road. Dingman eventually becomes Shelter Valley Road, which winds very prettily through Vernonville and back down to Highway 2 at Grafton.

Hike off your Warkworth lunch at Goodrich-Loomis Conservation Area.

EAST

Explore Peterborough

Beyond the attractions in this entry, there are more than enough ways to fill the day in this leafy riverside city. It's a great place to tour by bicycle, with a good choice of country roads with light traffic that are easily accessible from town. There is also a banquet of options for waterside picnicking in the area.

But the first stop on the trip should be an unprepossessing factory building in the town's unlovely south end. Don't be put off: the Canadian Canoe Museum inside is a treasure.

The Canadian Canoe Museum

Once famed as English-speaking Canada's most typical city and now becoming a post-industrial retirement centre, Peterborough retains one undiminished claim to quintessential Canadiana: It is the home of the canoe, the poetic vehicle that made this country in the first place and remains the prime symbol of its romantic imagination.

Peterborough's claim rests on two bases, the first being the genius of pioneer craftsmen in the valley of the

The Coppermine Expedition, 19
L'expédition de Coppermine, 19

Otonabee River, who adapted the Indigenous technology to industrial production and created the "white man's canoe," which quickly displaced the birchbark canoe in practical use and opened new frontiers for recreation. Local builders, led by the Peterborough Canoe Company, ultimately created the famous cedarstrip canoe, which they exported worldwide. The second is the Canadian Canoe Museum, a wonderful institution in the making that already occupies a top spot on any list of second-tier cultural attractions in the country.

You might think that a handful of canoes would be more than enough to satisfy your curiosity, let alone the many dozens you are sure to encounter here, but the collection is so diverse — and so well contextualized with other artifacts, historical settings and explanatory panels — that you might well wish for more. The museum features Peterborough as a prominent centre of canoe history and more than justifies its claim as essential Canadiana.

Kid-focused activities include a puppet theatre, canoe craft station and building table, reading nook, a voyager encampment and dress-up area and a 5-metre canoe drum!

A gorgeous new building planned for the bank of the Trent-Severn Waterway, next to the famous Peterborough Lift Lock, promises to make this model museum spectacular. And speaking of lift locks, you've come to the right place…

Explanatory panels, pictures and artifacts elevate the exhibits at the Canadian Canoe Museum.

The historic Peterborough Lift Lock.

Peterborough Lift Lock

Peterborough is home to the world's tallest example of this rare hydraulic type, a National Historic Site and engineering marvel that still impresses more than a century after its construction in 1904, all the more as it becomes increasingly historic. Its enormous, gleaming hydraulic rams, each more than 2 metres wide and 20 metres tall, silently lift and lower the weight of 30 elephants (or powerboats) using the power of gravity alone.

Enjoy the visitors' centre on site and picnic on the grounds.

It's a great way to relax with kids while watching for boats to come and go.

Historic Downtown

Downtown Peterborough has held up well despite this small city's steady loss of the manufacturing jobs that once made it hop. It survives in no small part because the city offers substantial property tax relief — the maximum allowed by provincial law — to owners of historically designated buildings. It's also far more entertaining these days, with lots of interesting new restaurants and cafés joining the beloved dive bars of yore, all still going strong, to make for a lively scene day and night.

The main drag, George Street, is handsome and well tenanted but caters more to the needs of locals than tourists. One exception is the Art Gallery of Peterborough, on Little Lake, which offers free admission.

The newly emerged Hunter Street café district, due west from the lift lock, offers first-class fare at places like the Planet Bakery at 374 Water Street and the Belgian-themed St. Veronus Café and Tap Room at 129 Hunter Street West. If you love books, stop by Hunter Street Books at No. 164, owned and operated by author Michelle Berry.

LIFTLOCK CRUISES
Peterborough's one-and-only party boat, the *Island Princess III*, has the entire Otonabee River to explore. Book in advance because the cruises are often sold out. See www.liftlockcruises.com.

The River Road Tour to Lakefield

This is a classic scenic route that begins in downtown Peterborough and follows the east bank of the Otonabee River 16 kilometres north to the pretty village of Lakefield. It's always worth driving — preferably with the top down and the sun shining — but it's an even better bike route, with lots of twists and no hills. Traffic is usually light, but there is also an off-road rail path that parallels the route. Well-maintained picnic sites are available at the locks, where pleasure boats pause on their journey up and down the river. This itinerary makes for an ideal family excursion.

The route begins in Peterborough's East City, just west of the lift lock, on Hunter Street East. For cyclists, from here the Rotary Greenway Trail heads north out of town. Access to the route is well indicated by signage. Drivers should follow Armour Road north and then turn right on Nassau Mills Road.

The first stop is Trent University, a masterpiece of modern architecture that has kept its special character over decades of additions and renovations. To experience the best of architect Ron Thom's original 1966 campus, stop here and cross the iconic Faryon Bridge on foot to visit Champlain College and the Bata Library on the western bank of the river.

Continuing north from Trent along the riverbank, County Road 32 passes three locks that enable pleasure boats to climb or descend the river, each set amid well-maintained picnic grounds, with washroom facilities available. These are the only federally funded amenities you will find in these pages (the waterway is maintained by Parks Canada), so you might as well take advantage.

As you will probably notice if you wind your way along the road during the summer, this stretch of the Otonabee is also a prime spot for shore fishing. Worms and bobbers are

LEFT
The Rotary Greenway Trail along the Otonabee River.

Trent University's Champlain College.

hardy English pub grub and the usual array of craft beer. Or you can pedal a bit farther north along Water Street and enjoy your own picnic in the waterside pavilion of Isabel Morris Park.

The Warsaw Caves Conservation Area

If you're driving — and especially if you have children aboard — consider a side trip to the Warsaw Caves Conservation Area on the banks of the Indian River. As its name indicates, the main draw here is an easily accessible network of underground caves that never fail to entertain young spelunkers. It also has one of the nicest small swimming beaches in the Kawarthas, where public beaches are scandalously rare, interesting hiking trails and canoe rentals available for an easy float down the river to the village of Warsaw. The area is located about 12 kilometres east of Lakefield, following County Road 6 and then south on County Road 4.

The tour to Lakefield ends with an ice cream from Stuff'd or a pint from the Canoe & Paddle, both at 18 Bridge Street.

perfect for this most casual form of angling.

For the generations of tourists, students and children who have cycled or driven this route, the ultimate goal remains unchanged: a Kawartha Dairy ice cream cone in Lakefield at the Bridge Street establishment once known as Hamlin's, now called Stuff'd. For more substantial fare, the Canoe and Paddle right next door serves

---

KAWARTHA CLASSICS CYCLING ROUTES

The competition among near-urban regions to attract weekend cyclists from the GTA is heating up nicely, with Niagara currently in the forefront, but Peterborough County is not far behind. Blessed with a rolling rural landscape criss-crossed by a network of lightly travelled paved roads, the region has done more to put cycling on the map, in the literal sense, than any other.

Working with local enthusiasts and a major corporate partner (Peterborough is the Canadian headquarters of Japanese cycling giant Shimano Inc.), the county established three scenic loops, each subdivided into one long and one short route, and erected no fewer than 160 prominent roadside signs to guide cyclists through every turn along all six routes.

The result is that you can venture deep into some of the province's best cycling terrain without even taking a map. Naturally, those are also widely available. Visit thekawarthas.ca/explore/cycling to read more about the routes and download the maps.

EAST

Time travel to Lang Pioneer Village

On the banks of the bucolic Indian River in southern Peterborough County, heavy glaciation has left a pattern of steep whale-backed hills, called drumlins, that stoutly impede human progress. Here you can spend a whole day visiting the Lang Pioneer Village and Museum, cycling local trails and picnicking amid ancient burial mounds on the shore of Rice Lake — and never leave the 19th century.

Lang Pioneer Village and Museum

Our world is not short of pioneer villages, but few are as authentic feeling as the Lang Pioneer Village and Museum, a rustic world apart settled deep into its rural landscape. The centre of attention here is the Lang Mill, three full storeys of cut stone still standing as straight and true as the day it was built in 1846. Across the river, the museum has gathered more than 30 other buildings, each containing artifacts, from throughout the county in an engaging and sometimes fascinating ensemble of early farm life in southern Ontario.

One of the many log cabins on the site was the home of David Fife, who in 1842 developed an early-maturing strain of wheat, known as Red Fife, that was key to turning the Canadian Prairies into one of the world's great breadbaskets. After all but disappearing in the 20th century, Red Fife has returned as "a principal icon of local food consumption and production in Ontario," according to one account.

Guides in period costumes demonstrate traditional chores and pastimes. Two rare Jacquard looms occupy a new shop and interpretative centre. Steam engines, stump pullers and honey

wagons decorate the gardens. For hours of operation and admission prices, visit langpioneervillage.ca.

Hope Mill

Just a few kilometres upriver from Lang sits another miraculous survivor. The Hope Mill is a working sawmill dating from 1836, where twin water-powered turbines turn wooden-toothed gears that distribute power through an elaborate system of belts and pulleys to a 1-metre circular saw snatched from the dreams of Snidely Whiplash. Hope Mill is open to visitors every Tuesday from mid-April to late October, from 9:30 a.m. to 4 p.m. Come and watch the heritage equipment cut and finish lumber, and visit the woodworking museum and archive. Handmade wooden crafts are available for sale. Visit hopemill.ca for more information.

 William Lang and his wife Jane (Stewart) Lang, after whom Lang Pioneer Village was named, arrived from Scotland in 1832, settled along the Indian River and built the Hope Mill, which was originally a wool mill.

Lang-Hastings Rail Trail

Just down the river a few kilometres, in the opposite direction from the Hope Mill, you will find the prettiest section of the newly improved Lang-Hastings rail trail. Unlike the impossibly steep and straight roads that carry the grid through this hilly countryside — and unlike many other flat and boring rail trails elsewhere in the province — this one winds scenically along the contours, closely embracing the landscape, with postcard views opening around every bend.

For an easy loop that makes the best of the local scenery, hike or ride the rail trail east from where it intersects with County Road 34, just south of Lang Village, then turn south on Settler's Line toward Rice Lake. Lunch can be had at Elmhirst's Resort on the shore, or you can follow Lakeside Road west to the pretty village of Keene, where Muddy's Pit BBQ serves giant racks of roasted meat.

Serpent Mounds

Even better would be a picnic at the Serpent Mounds, a famous archaeological site 4 kilometres south of Keene on the Rice Lake shore. The mounds

The Serpent Mounds and a view of Rice Lake.

are burial tumuli dating back 2,000 years, the largest of which is a sinuous landform in the shape of a snake. They are the only effigy mounds (mounds in the shape of animals or symbols) that have been discovered in Canada. The setting is beautiful: a rolling oak savannah giving lovely views of the lake and its wooded islands, with a small sandy beach at the shore.

Once a provincial park replete with campsites and swimming beaches, Serpent Mounds was taken over 20 years ago by its landlord, the adjoining Hiawatha First Nation, and subsequently closed pending redevelopment. However, respectful visitors are generally welcome.

MILLBROOK AND 4TH LINE THEATRE

Looking to mix some outdoor theatre with your historical tour? For the last 26 years, the **4th Line Theatre** has been bringing history to life on stage at the rustic **Winslow Farm**, near Millbrook. The 4th Line Theatre is "committed to preserving our Canadian cultural heritage through the development and presentation of environmentally staged historical drama." Bring your own packed lunch to eat at the farm before the show, or pre-order a picnic spread online to enjoy when you arrive.

EAST

Birdwatch in Presqu'ile Provincial Park

Spring can be a dreary time in old Ontario: a long interval of bad weather after the blanket comes off the land but during which nature continues to slumber, only to jolt awake in mid-May with the sudden onset of summer. It's a hard time to enjoy the outdoors, but also the time winter-weary Canadians most need to get out. So if you're not going to Florida, consider a trip to Presqu'ile Provincial Park to enjoy one of the province's great bird-watching opportunities: the spring waterfowl migration. Don't shy away from visiting at other times of the year, too.

For the Birds

Like Long Point and Point Pelee on the north shore of Lake Erie, Lake Ontario's Presqu'ile juts far enough south to be a favoured landing and staging place for birds migrating over the lakes. Although much smaller than Long Point, it has a diversity of habitats that attract and hold hundreds of different kinds of birds. It's not uncommon for avid birders to record 100 or more species in a single day at Presqu'ile. But it's never as crowded as Pelee and is closer to Toronto than Long Point.

• Spring Migration: Waterfowl and Songbirds

The high season for birders here stretches throughout spring until the trees leaf out in May. However, the opening event — the appearance of thousands of ducks, geese and swans in the marshes of Presqu'ile Bay — has a special appeal.

The waterfowl begin to appear in March and cluster near the edge of the ice as it melts away from the shore, making them easy to see and photograph. If all you've ever seen is a mallard or two in High Park, you will be astonished by the variety and colours of scaups, scoters, widgeons, pintails and canvasbacks you can closely observe in the bay — as many as 25 different species on a single visit, according to park naturalists. May brings songbirds in equal abundance.

• Fall Migration: Shorebirds

The fall migration at Presqu'ile is famous for shorebirds, which are easy to spot as they scoot about the beach. Twenty-five species of shorebird make annual stops here, and more than 40 have been recorded over the years. The best time to see them is September, after most of the shore humans have gone for the year.

Birdwatching and photographing are two of Presqu'ile's main draws.

Sanderlings are among the shorebirds you can spot at Presqu'ile during the fall migration.

The original lighthouse-keeper's cottage is now the site for the Lighthouse Interpretive Centre.

Lighthouse Interpretive Centre

Presqu'ile is home to the second-oldest lighthouse on the shores of Lake Ontario. Located at the end of Lighthouse Lane, the Lighthouse Interpretive Centre incorporates the original lighthouse-keeper's cottage. Here you can learn about the history of the lighthouse, the notorious shipwreck nearby and the outlaw rum-running days of old. The centre is open 10 a.m. to 5 p.m. every day between Canada Day and Labour Day and 10 a.m. to 4 p.m. on weekends in the spring and fall. Also along Lighthouse Lane, you'll find the Nature Interpretive Centre, which explores biodiversity

BIRDING GUIDES AND RESOURCES

Your birding trip will be more interesting if you know what you are looking for:

- The Nature Interpretive Centre has a library of field guides.
- For an online guide, search "Willow Beach field naturalists" and "birds of Northumberland County."
- The Friends of Presqu'ile Park has provided an online checklist so you can keep track of your sightings.
- Lone Pine Publishing puts out the "Quick Reference to Ontario Birds," a laminated fold-out 12 panel guide featuring 83 of Ontario's most common and interesting birds.
- Looking for something comprehensive? You have several choices. Birds Ontario published *The Atlas of Breeding Birds of Ontario*, available to order for $60 from their website. A cheaper option is the *Lorimer Field Guide to 225 Ontario Birds*, at $20.

Summer at Presqu'ile is a different matter. It's meant for swimming and sunning on one of Lake Ontario's longest beaches. It's almost an hour closer than the more popular Sandbanks Provincial Park in Prince Edward County, so it's a much better choice for a day trip.

in the park with live examples of frogs, reptiles and fish, as well as a hands-on Ordovician fossil display — a big hit with kids.

Nearby Brighton

If birdwatching and beach-lazing are too tame for you, organized mayhem is easily obtained right next door to Presqu'ile at the Brighton Speedway, where country people from all over Ontario and beyond convene to practise their traditional folkways — in this case, racing cars fender to fender and sideways around a tiny dirt track on a quiet summer evening. It's loud, dirty, bad for the planet but undeniably fun. The Speedway stages a full slate of races every Saturday evening from April to September, with grids of stock cars and sprint cars that cover half the track even before the start. It's a true contact sport, but the speeds are never high enough to hurt anyone. The

Brighton Speedway is located at 775 County Road 64, just east of Presqu'ile Provincial Park.

Downtown Brighton is a day-tripper's destination in its own right. After some antiquing at End of the Thread Emporium at 13 Main Street and shopping at the Blue House at No. 79, enjoy a latte at Lola's Coffee House, located at 74 Main.

Brighton Speedway is roaring good fun on an all-dirt track.

EAST

Sample a *Prince Edward County* WINE TOUR

Waupoos Estate Winery in Prince Edward County.

The skyline is only one hint of how Toronto has grown during the 21st century. For another perspective, consider the emergence of Prince Edward County (PEC) as a major tourist destination with an international reputation for fine wine and dining. At the turn of the century, this large peninsula was the most bypassed backwater in southern Ontario, its thin soils worked out and half-abandoned more than a century ago and its beaches and cottages a poor-man's substitute for the more desirable locales in the north country. Today, it is the hippest getaway destination in the country — "a global hot spot," according to *Travel+Leisure* magazine — totally made over by urban exiles with urban money and the urban tourists who followed their lead.

Unlike that other peninsula across the lake, "the county" is a bit distant for easy day trips from Toronto. Google Maps optimistically calculates the driving time between the Drake Hotel in Toronto and the Drake Devonshire in Wellington, epicentre of the new rural hipness, at 2 hours and 17 minutes. Most vacationers here will stay overnight at least. But if you've ever enjoyed a wine tour in Niagara, you'll find a lot to like in its more rustic upstart relative.

Rise of the Wineries

The instrument of PEC's revival was made possible by a fortuitous combination of global warming and the same stony limestone soil — not great for crops, but terrific for vines — that once led so many farms into decline. More than 40 wineries have appeared in fewer than 20 years, buoyed by a steady tide of favourable publicity about this marvellous new discovery (that is actually one of the oldest settled places in Upper Canada). Although their output is small even by Canadian standards, together they have pioneered an entirely new tourist economy.

Organized Tours: The Way to Go

Given the amount of driving involved, both to get there and to travel between wineries, an organized tour is the most sensible approach for a day on the wine route in the county.

◆ Tours from Toronto

Tours from Toronto offer door-to-door convenience.

- **New World Wine Tours** offers a full-day tour, 10 hours long, that leaves from the downtown hotels and includes a pizza lunch at the popular Norman Hardie Winery. Visit newworldwinetours.com.
- **Toronto Food Tours** leads a similar expedition every Saturday during the warm months, leaving from the Distillery District. See tofoodtours.com.

If you have a designated driver and want to plan your own tour, the **Prince Edward County Winegrowers Association** publishes all the information you need, plus an interactive map that you can customize and print out as an itinerary. See princeedwardcountywine.ca.

- **The County Wine Tours** offers the area's only bicycle wine tour. See thecountywinetours.com.
- **County Sips** is led by sommelier Ian Nicholls. See countysips.com.
- **Sandbanks Vacations and Tours** offers half- and full-day guided tours as well as private wine tours. See sandbanksvacations.com.
- In addition to tour packages, **Prince Edward County Wine Tours** has accommodation packages, in case you decide to stay a couple of days. See pecwinetours.com.
- **Spotlight Limousine** offers private tours for up to eight people with knowledgeable drivers. See spotlightlimousine.ca.

With over 40 wineries and a growing tourist industry, Prince Edward County may one day rival Niagara's wine region.

◆ Tours from Within the County

More companies operate within the county itself, catering to weekenders and summer vacationers. Thanks to VIA Rail, you can easily join them for a day trip, drink as much as you like and not have to drive anywhere. An early train leaves Union Station at 6:40 a.m. every day except Sunday (the earliest train on Sunday leaves at 9:20 a.m.), arriving two hours later in Belleville, where local tour operators will pick you up. There's a choice of return trains in the evening. Here are some of the companies that offer wine tours from within the county:

TERROIR SPRING WINE AND FOOD FESTIVAL

Terroir, the winegrower's annual spring festival, takes place in mid-May and brings together the county's leading wineries, restaurants, food producers and farmers at the historic **Crystal Palace** in **Picton**. With more than 20 wineries participating, this is an excellent opportunity to find the best the county has to offer — and to plan future excursions to favoured spots. In late September, the group returns to the Crystal Palace with a second culinary festival and marketplace called **TASTE community grown**. See princeedwardcountywine.ca for details.

EAST

Ride the Prince Edward County

CYCLING ROUTES

Cyclists in Prince Edward County should expect routes through a lot of serene countryside.

Clocking in at over two hours, the drive to Prince Edward County (PEC) is an ambitious one for day trippers, and you have to drive through a lot of prime cycling terrain to reach your destination, but the effort is worth making. There's nowhere else in the province that has the same combination of scenic back roads with a deep rural feel and ultra-modern roadside attractions — wineries with their tasting bars, restaurants, galleries and boutiques. Then, of course, there are the best beaches on Lake Ontario.

Bloomfield Bicycle Company has everything for a PEC cycling adventure.

Road (County Road 1) from Picton to Consecon and Highway 49 from Picton to Deseronto.

Bloomfield Bicycle Company

The most authoritative source of information about cycling in Prince Edward County is the long-established, well-stocked and slightly eccentric Bloomfield Bicycle Company, located in the village of the same name at 225 Main Street (Highway 33). In addition to doing repairs and selling all manner of cycling supplies, the company maintains a fleet of good-quality bikes for hire by the day. It also distributes a free map of recommended routes. This shop is an all-analogue experience, and if you go so far as to deploy a cell phone while browsing, you will be reproved. Read the signs! And don't complain. The map is worth it.

Because the county's road network was originally laid out in the late 18th century, before the Imperial gridiron descended upon the Upper Canadian landscape, roads here meander in response to geography rather than opposed to it, and there's a lot of geography here: jagged points and deep bays, lakes, spits, beaches and coves, but not much in the way of hills. It's perfect for cycling.

You'll need a map, but not necessarily a plan, as there are back-road routes connecting every point in the county. At the same time, there can be a lot of traffic on the main routes, especially during the summer. Roads to avoid include Highway 62 south from Belleville to Bloomfield, Scoharie

After you return by bike, end your trip with a local meal: **Agrarian Bistro** at 275 Main Street in Bloomfield is a good option, and so is **East & Main** in Wellington. Looking for ice cream? **Slickers** on Main Street in Bloomfield has a great selection of homemade flavours and a nice seating area outside.

Three Cycling Routes

Beginning at Bloomfield, three basic routes, each with variations, are open to the day tripper. The first two give you the option of a beach visit. The third tours a little-visited corner of the northern county.

• The Hillier Wine Route

Heading west from Bloomfield takes you through the heart of the county's wine district, past Wellington toward the hamlet of Hillier. The fastest way to get there is to follow Highway 33, which has narrow paved shoulders but lots of traffic, especially on summer weekends. As an alternative, you can ride the off-road Millennium Trail all the way to Hillier, although its loose gravel surface is not for everyone.

Both routes lead to the village of Wellington, home to some of the oldest buildings in Ontario and one of its hippest novelties: the Drake Devonshire Inn. Unless you book in advance, you won't be stopping here. And if you do reserve a table for lunch, you might not get much farther along the route.

The Grange of Prince Edward winery can be found along Closson Road.

If wine is your goal, you can ride north 6 kilometres on County Road 2 to the intersection of Closson Road, the Golden Mile of the county wine district. You'll pass a dozen wineries heading west on Closson and then Danforth Road (a trace of the original 18th century trail connecting Kingston and Toronto) toward Hillier. But be warned: this is one of the bumpiest "paved" roads in the county. You can also get to Hillier by continuing to follow either Highway 33 or the Millennium Trail.

OTHER CYCLING SHOPS

E-bikes are an increasingly popular option for casual cyclists, and there are now two shops in the county where you can rent bikes that will whisk you effortlessly up the few hills you are likely to encounter here. **Pedego Electric Bikes** does business at 39 Stanley Street in Bloomfield, while **East Lake Electric Bike** can be found on County Road 11 near Sandbanks. Belleville's **Ideal Bike** operates a branch in Wellington, while **Closson Road Cycles** offers rentals in the heart of the Hillier wine district.

The tempting, picturesque beaches of Sandbanks Provincial Park.

Just south of Hillier is another cluster of wineries, anchored by the popular Norman Hardie Winery and pizza patio. You can find a map at princeedwardcountywine.ca to help sort the possibilities for tasting and dining here.

If you've ridden to Hillier along Highway 33, you can loop around by heading southeast on Danforth Road then following the colourfully named Swamp College and Gilead Roads until you hit Highway 62. Follow that road south to return to Bloomfield, but be careful of traffic. Indigo Skymind of the Bloomfield Bicycle Co. suggests riding the loop counter-clockwise, returning on Highway 33 to avoid the worst of the wind. In either case, the entire trip is about 40 kilometres.

If it's summertime, consider riding another few kilometres west to **North Beach Provincial Park**. Much smaller and less popular than Sandbanks to the south, North Beach somehow manages to remain the archetypal hidden gem. It's natural and pristine with diamond-clear water.

◆ Sandbanks Route

Sandbanks Provincial Park is still the main event in Prince Edward County and has been for generations of vacationers from the pre-hipster era. This is unquestionably the best beach on either side of Lake Ontario, with clear shallow water for kilometres and spectacular high dunes that are unique in the province. It also rivals Wasaga Beach (pages 51–54) for crowds, especially on weekends, but the looping roads you can follow to get there traverse a timeless rural landscape, with nary a winery in sight.

The tour is outlined in pink on the free map available from Bloomfield Bicycle Company. If you ride it counter-clockwise, you'll hit the beach early and leave most of the riding until later; clockwise will warm you up with a long, lovely spin before the beach, followed by a short trip back to Bloomfield. In either case, you'll find that cycling is the ideal way to penetrate the crowds and bypass a parking crush that can cut hours from your beach time at Sandbanks.

The fastest way to the beach is to cycle the route counter-clockwise. Follow the winding Shannon Road south from Bloomfield for 4.5 kilometres. Turn left (south) on Marisett Road and follow it until you reach County Road 11, which lines the north shore of East Lake. Sandbanks' entrance is 5 kilometres west on County Road 11.

The long route back to Bloomfield takes you southward on County Road 18 and then connects to Wellbanks Road. Ride Wellbanks for 2 kilometres, then turn left (east) onto Kelly Road. Follow the zig-zagging Kelly Road east and north to Brummell Road, which links to County Road 10. Riding east on County Road 10 brings you to the pretty hamlet of Milford. From here you can either follow an eastern loop through Black River, as indicated on the map, or take a shortcut north on bumpy Old Milford Road. The alternate routes eventually relink at the intersection of Old Milford Road and McKinley Crossroad. Continue on Old Milford until it becomes Kingsley Road, and then ride Kingsley until it ends at Picton Airport. From there, turn south (left) on Church Street (County Road 22) and follow it to County Road 10. A short jog north brings you to Ridge Road, which winds west back to Shannon Road, just south of Bloomfield.

The catch on this route is summer traffic, which can make the pleasantest back roads in the vicinity of the

EXPLORING SANDBANKS

One of the best reasons to visit Sandbanks by bike is that cyclists enjoy free entry. There are also bike racks installed throughout the park. Before you go swimming, you should ride either the new **Lakeview Trail** that traces the rocky point separating the two beach areas or the **Woodlands Trail**. Sandbanks also offers several short hikes, including the **Sandbanks Dunes Trail**, a 2.5-kilometre loop around a unique and fragile dune habitat. Kayaks and canoes are available for rent, and there are also several restaurants and picnic shelters in the park.

The hops from Winddance Stables and Farm go to breweries and distilleries across the province.

park hazardous. This suggested route sneaks around the worst of it, but the closer you get to the beach the heavier the traffic becomes.

◆ Big Island Route

Most of northern PEC is so sparsely visited it might as well not exist, but the trip up to and around Big Island offers the best shoreline cycling in the county, according to local cycling sage Indigo Skymind of the Bloomfield Bicycle Co. You won't find many other tourists or wineries or boutiques on this route. The attraction is North Big Island Road, a narrow paved path that runs right beside the Bay of Quinte for several kilometres, with no cottages or other properties between it and the shore. It's the quietest, most scenic cycling road in the county.

Follow County Road 30 north out of Bloomfield to County Road 4, the Old Belleville Road, then head west on 4 to Doxsee Road. Turn north (right) on Doxsee and follow it until you hit the shore of the Bay of Quinte. Turn right (east) onto County Road 14, which takes you to the faded hamlet of Demorestville. From there follow County Roads 15 and 21 north to reach Big Island. The scenic tour around the island is 18 kilometres. Along the way you'll pass the Winddance Stables and Farm at 1166 North Big Island Road, which grows towering hops plants to supply the province's burgeoning craft beer industry and also sells custom canes and walking sticks.

To return to Bloomfield, follow County Road 5 south from Demorestville to Fry Road, then travel in a straight line southwest along Fry, May and Mallory (County Road 32) back to town. The total route is an easy 50 kilometres.

The Bloomfield Bicycle Company map shows how to get there and back from Bloomfield, but you can sample the best of the ride by parking your car in Demorestville and circling the island from there.

GO Transit Cycle Tours

Most people who like to explore the country around Toronto by bike begin their journeys by car. It's practical but by no means the only way to go. The steady increase in regional transit services has opened up some easy and flexible options for those who either don't have cars or prefer not to use them on cycling trips. Taking transit also extends the number of routes available to ride by enabling you to start at one point and end at another.

Frequent weekend service on the GO Transit Lakeshore line makes a carless bike tour possible. There is always a train coming and almost always room aboard for bicycles (except during weekday rush hours, when they are not allowed). There are plenty of options for circuits looping off the main line that require little or no planning, and the number of routes you can plot is limitless if you take GO buses into account and care to consult schedules.

Starting at Union Station can turn a familiar morning ride into something completely different.

Routes East

The most obvious choice for the casual cyclist is the Great Lakes Waterfront Trail, which parallels the rail line from Oshawa to Hamilton and the Niagara Region. It's so obvious that trail organizers have partnered with local authorities to map a system of the best low-traffic routes connecting 11 GO stations and the trail. Simply follow the "Trail to GO" signs to find your way.

The eastern section of the Waterfront Trail past Scarborough is especially nice. It can be cycled all at once

starting in Oshawa and ending back in Toronto, or by subdividing the route into smaller sections. The mainly off-road trail from Oshawa west to Rouge Hill station in Scarborough is about 40 kilometres long — 50 kilometres if you stretch it along the bluffs to Guildwood.

Rouge Hill station is a particularly sweet spot for cyclists. It's located immediately adjacent to a long, off-road section of the trail through eastern Scarborough and into the wilds of Pickering. It's like a hidden back door into the big city. Your best bet is to ride this section of the trail early in the morning to avoid the crowds of pedestrians that appear every sunny afternoon. See waterfronttrail.org for route details.

For those seeking more challenging tours, Oshawa and Ajax are the places to jump off. From the Ajax GO station, a 20-kilometre trip north on Westney Road takes you out of town and into the rolling countryside near Glen Major Conservation Area (see pages 135–8).

The route north through Oshawa is better, following bike lanes most of the way, but not before passing through some nastiness. To find it, ride west on Victoria Street from the GO station to Thickson Road, north 1.5 kilometres on Thickson, over the 401, to Burns Street. Turn east (right) on Burns and north on Kendalwood Road. Kendalwood turns into Garrard Road, which heads north into the hills.

The Durham Cycling Club's Tart Ride is a good example of the kind of touring to expect here. It's a 65-kilometre circuit from downtown Oshawa that gradually climbs the moraine, tortures you up there for a spell and then blessedly descends back to the lake. The object of the quest is butter tarts at Hy-Hope Farm near Dagmar. See durhamcycling.com, where you can search for details of that route and dozens of others in the region.

Routes West

The Great Lakes Waterfront Trail west of Toronto is more consistently urbanized than its eastern counterpart, but it has the advantage of connecting directly to the central city. Rather than starting with a train ride to get through Scarborough, you can more easily cycle all the way out and then ride the rails home. The one-way tour from the Humber River to Aldershot station in Burlington is an easy 60 kilometres, passing through Port Credit and Oakville along the way. Aldershot station is also a short ride away from the Royal Botanical Gardens (see pages 79–82).

Getting into the enticing country north of Burlington begins with a gruelling, 4-kilometre climb up the escarpment along Waterdown Road to the town of the same name. An easier way to explore the same area is to start in Georgetown. GO buses travel there regularly from various pick-up points in Toronto, and each bus is equipped with a rack that carries two bicycles. Follow the Greenbelt Route back down (being the operative word) to Aldershot. It's a lovely rural tour of about 60 kilometres along lightly travelled roads and is easily extendable by following the Greenbelt Route farther west into the Dundas Valley and looping back through Hamilton along the Waterfront Trail.

Georgetown is also a good place to begin an exploration of the upper Credit Valley (pages 27–31). See greenbelt.ca/explore for details on riding in the area.

Routes South

For cycling in the Niagara Region, there is GO Transit's Niagara Bike Train, a seasonal service that caters specifically to cyclists' needs and wants. See pages 97–101 to read more about the service and recommended routes around the Niagara Peninsula.

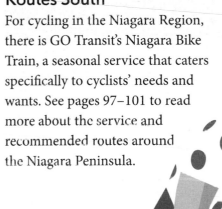

WEST

If you travel straight west from Toronto, you will soon enter a farmer's paradise of flat land, large fields and few trees that stretches monotonously ahead for hundreds of kilometres. For the rest of us, the good stuff is much closer: a varied terrain along the spine of the Niagara Escarpment and crossways down the valley of the historic Grand River, which creates an intricate geography adorned with the most picturesque old mill towns in the province. The village of Elora could take the prize as the best day-trip destination out of Toronto, rivalled by nearby St. Jacobs, long a magnet for urbanites with a taste for Mennonite "food that really schmecks."

Some of the most attractive destinations, like the parks of Halton Region, are so close they're almost suburban. Others, like the Stratford Festival, repay the extra travel required to reach them with extraordinary experiences. Generally speaking, however, these destinations are as easily reachable as they are rewarding. Stray too far and the world gets boring pretty fast; stay close by and it's full of interest.

Jet off to the Great War Flying Museum

What drives grown men to devote countless hours to the painstaking reconstruction and maintenance of ancient aeroplanes (as they are known to members of the Great War Flying Museum) made of fabric, wood and chewing gum? "We don't know exactly why," they say on their website. "It's a very regulated, demanding and expensive hobby. But we love it."

Passion over reason is the motto here, and the feeling is infectious. The early "Knights of the Air" had a life expectancy measured in days, and their aircraft were equally expendable, but the romance of their exploits is impossible to deny.

Authentic Aeroplanes and Artifacts

The museum maintains a fully flight-worthy fleet of six World War I aircraft, including replicas of fighters flown by the famous Red Baron, Manfred von Richthofen; leading U.S. ace Eddie Rickenbacker; and Canadians Billy Bishop and George Barker, both recipients of the Victoria Cross for their airborne heroics. The frames are made of welded steel rather than

wood and the engines are modern, but only an expert could distinguish the differences. The museum is such a stickler for authenticity that it repainted its replica of the Red Baron's bright red Fokker triplane to match the less striking colours it actually wore in combat.

In addition to the planes, the museum displays a small collection of everyday artifacts and equipment associated with the earliest fighter pilots.

This trip is not only family friendly, it's easy on the budget, too. Admission is by donation and parking is free.

◆ Before You Visit

The museum is open to the public on weekends and holidays from Victoria Day until Labour Day. Be sure to check its website under "Upcoming Events" to confirm the planes will be on hand when you plan to be there: No hangar queens, they're in demand for air shows and often flying about.

You can also visit the hangar Tuesdays and Thursdays to watch aircrews repair and maintain the aircraft.

The Great War Flying Museum's replica of Eddie Rickenbacker's Nieuport 28.

Want to prep your young ones for the visit? *Those Magnificent Men in Their Flying Machines*, a slapstick-style comedy based on a historic 1910 airplane race across the English Channel, is full of aerobatic stunts in vintage airplanes that will pique their interest.

The Great War Flying Museum is under 30 minutes from the **Credit River Valley** and **Caledon** region, which is great for hiking, cycling or a scenic drive (see pages 27–31).

In return for a $200 membership, you can take a ride in the museum's Sopwith Strutter, the only two-seat plane in its collection.

Breakfast and lunch are available at the Brampton Flying Club's Wings Flight Grille, and the airport gift shop is open to the public.

The museum's replica planes are flightworthy and often appear in air shows.

SAMOSAS IN BRAMPTON

It is a fact universally acknowledged that anybody driving through Brampton must stop for samosas. They may be stone cold by the time you get home, but all Torontonians respect the authentic made-in-Brampton samosa. Better still to stop for a full meal here, home of some of the best, most varied Indian food on the continent. But like the bagel in Montreal, the samosa is the ambassador that best embodies the emerging culinary identity of this intensely multicultural sprawl.

If your new-restaurant radar directs you to places most crowded with people who appear to be local, you may well end up at **Kwality Sweets** at 2150 Steeles Avenue East. It's one of the most popular Indian restaurants in Brampton and does a booming sit-down as well as take-home business.

They may have moved across the line to Mississauga, but "the experts in English style samosa" at **A-One Catering** have emerged as the region's leading samosa exporters from their new wholesale factory located at 7875 Tranmere Drive in an industrial park just north of Pearson airport.

The **Indian Punjabi Bazaar** is mainly a grocery store, but it also sells prepared meals and snacks, including samosas of great repute. You'll find it in a strip mall on the east side of McLaughlin Street South, just north of Highway 407 and south of Ray Lawson Boulevard (499 Ray Lawson Boulevard).

Get outdoors in the Halton Parks

Laid like a green blanket over the western entrance to the GTA, the cluster of parks operated by Conservation Halton on either side of Highway 401 are very close to the city. They could easily be considered suburban, having been developed to a degree you won't often find in other conservation areas. But they are big enough to afford genuine outdoor experiences, and the escarpment they straddle is one of the province's most scenic landscapes. Most of all, they are close enough that visiting here can be an easy alternative to yet another stroll through the local ravines.

Rattlesnake Point

This is the most prominent of the Halton Parks, in every sense: a landmark lookout, called Buffalo Crag, once served sailors who jumped ship in Hamilton and then camped here until they could see their former workplaces

For the very affordable price of admission, you can visit any of the Halton Parks, which are all within a very short distance of each other. Pack a lunch and make a day of it!

Visitors can try their hand at rock climbing exposed limestone cliffs.

safely sailing out of the harbour, 20 kilometres away. There are 12 kilometres of colour-coded trails here, with short loops that take in the best views. Watch for turkey vultures and observe the ancient cedars, some over 800 years old, growing from the cliff face.

For those who want more than views, the exposed limestone cliffs of the escarpment have made this Ontario's most popular rock-climbing destination. Both Zen Climb (zenclimb.com) and Adventure Seeker Tours (adventureseekertours.com) offer a number of courses to both novice and advanced climbers at Rattlesnake Point.

Parking is available at 7200 Appleby Line, Milton.

Crawford Lake Conservation Area

Directly adjoining Rattlesnake Point to the west, the Crawford Lake Conservation Area is a family-oriented park with a gift shop, organized activities and an archaeologically correct reconstruction of a pre-contact 15th-century Iroquoian village, with three of the

NASSAGAWEYA CANYON TRAIL

If you want to explore two parks in one without getting back in your car, the **Nassagaweya Canyon Trail** is a terrific hike that starts at **Crawford Lake** and ascends **Rattlesnake Point** more than 4 kilometres later, offering a far more satisfying introduction to the heights than you can get at the edge of a parking lot. It's an out-and-back affair, meaning it has no loops, making for a substantial 15-kilometre trek. It's especially beautiful in the fall.

original eleven longhouses built on the excavated foundations of the original buildings. Excavations also uncovered over 10,000 artifacts from the village. Displays, interpretive programs and traditional children's games further bring the village to life. The Deer Clan Longhouse features seasonal contemporary art exhibits from local First Nations artists. When you're finished at the village, take a self-guided hike around Crawford Lake. Parking is available near 3115 Conservation Road in Milton.

Glen Eden and Kelso Conservation Area

The adjoining Glen Eden ski hill and Kelso Conservation Area are the most developed parks in the system, the former attracting skiers and boarders and the latter a mountain-biking

nexus. The ski area is tiny, with a busy railway track cutting it in half, but it's well equipped to serve beginners. The cycling scene is more intense, with a number of important races held at Kelso throughout the season. There are 22 kilometres of marked trails, equipment rentals and cycling programs for children. Splash around or wade in the water with your kids, set up beach chairs or play beach volleyball. There's also a concession stand at the beach. For a cooler experience, rent a canoe, kayak or paddleboard and putter around Kelso Lake as traffic roars by

There are plenty of cycling opportunities in the Halton Parks, as well as some lovely vistas to bike to.

LEFT
A trail surrounds serene Crawford Lake.

The other Halton Parks are **Mount Nemo, Mountsberg** and **Robert Edmondson.** Visit conservationhalton.ca for more information.

The Hilton Falls waterfall is the reward at the end of a hike through forestland.

on the old '01. Access to both areas is located at 5234 Kelso Road.

Hilton Falls

Not many people east of Milton have ever heard of the Hilton Falls, a surprisingly large tract of undisturbed forestland just north of the 401, across from its sister parks. Although it lacks panoramic views, its 16-kilometre trail network is popular with hikers, cyclists, snowshoers and skiers. You might find park staff tending a bonfire at the stunning waterfall. If you are hiking in winter, bring birdseed to feed the chickadees at the falls. Find parking and trailheads at 4985 Campbellville Road.

Mattamy National Cycling Centre

Milton, the most recently transformed village-turned-technopolis on the western frontier of the ever-expanding

WINTER INTERLUDES

Halton Parks' trails are great for winter hikes. Cross-country ski trails are available at Crawford Lake, Hilton Falls and Mountsberg conservation areas. Rentals are available at Hilton Falls, where the trails are groomed. Snowshoeing is available at Crawford Lake and Mountsberg, and snowshoe rentals are available at Crawford Lake.

GTA, now has a world-class attraction to match its elevated status.

Built for the 2015 Pan Am Games, the Mattamy National Cycling Centre is the only indoor cycling track in Canada certified to host top-flight international events. It's also freely available to the public, with numerous opportunities for newcomers and casual riders to experience the peculiar thrill of a velodrome. See mattamynationalcyclingcentre.ca for program details. The centre is located at 2015 Pan Am Boulevard, just west of Tremaine Road.

The Mattamy National Cycling Centre.

APPLE PICKING AND PIES

It began in 1967 as a simple enough proposition: "a place where families could pick their own apples and savour a few hours of country life," according to the proprietors. Soon they began baking apple pies to sell. Today, **Chudleigh's** operates a 10,200-square-metre factory in Milton employing 200 workers and ships its baked goods all over North America. However, you can still visit the farm to pick apples in season, and thousands do. Chudleigh's currently grows 20 different varieties of apples and publishes a schedule estimating when each one will be ripe for picking. There's also a play area with wagon and pony rides throughout the picking season (beginning in mid-August), as well as an on-site bakery and store. The farm is located at 9528 Regional Road 25, about 5 kilometres north of Highway 401.

WEST

Explore *Guelph*

Guelph has the distinction of being one of the only cities in Canada (or anywhere, probably) founded by a novelist. And the influence of John Galt, a Scottish writer famous in his day, is immediately apparent the moment you descend into the Speed River Valley and enter the town. Along with the town of Goderich on Lake Huron — also laid out by Galt in his role as superintendent of the Canada Company — Guelph is the only city in the province that shows the slightest imagination in its plan, which deviates so dramatically from the standard-issue gridiron. The domineering presence of the Basilica of Our Lady Immaculate at the head of Macdonell Street, Guelph's own Notre Dame, heightens the hidden romance.

Hidden it mostly remains and, in that, Guelph is typically Ontarian. But that's no bad thing. Prosperous Guelph is consistently named one of the top places to live in Canada. It is no tourist mecca, but it nevertheless has much to offer both the accidental and the determined urban explorer.

Basilica of Our Lady Immaculate

You can take it all in from the steps of the basilica, Guelph's one claim to a "must-see" attraction. Granting the deed to the property to the Catholic Church in 1827, Galt grandly prophesized that "on this hill would one day rise a church to rival St. Peter's in Rome." The result came a lot closer to it than anything his most skeptical listener would have imagined. Masses are well attended every Sunday in the recently restored church, located at 28 Norfolk Street, and guided tours are offered Sunday afternoons. See basilicaofourlady.com for details.

Museums

While you're exploring the basilica, it only makes sense to pop into the Guelph Civic Museum, located in a former monastery on the church grounds. It's an immersive hodgepodge

The Guelph Civic Museum, near the Basilica.

ABOVE
The Basilica of Our Lady Immaculate.

of all things Guelph, with more than 30,000 items in its collection and digitized online.

The poet and surgeon John McCrae, author of "In Flanders Fields," is commemorated at his birthplace, McCrae House, across the river at 108 Water Street, a 15-minute walk from the Basilica and Guelph Civic Museum. It's often the site of informative exhibits and events.

Possibly the most intriguing museum in Guelph is the privately operated Hammond Museum of Radio, located at 595 Southgate Road in an industrial park south of town. Various Hammond companies have been manufacturing electronic components in Guelph for more than a century, and the museum took shape from a collection that company executive Fred Hammond began in the 1920s. It includes hundreds of receivers, transmitters and assorted tube-era paraphernalia, bewildering to most people but impressive nonetheless. The museum is open weekdays from 9 a.m. to 4 p.m. If you wish to visit on a weekend, contact the curator at 519-822-2441.

The Arboretum

Guelph has a fine set of parks along the Speed River adjacent to downtown, but the Arboretum at the University of Guelph is exceptional. Established in 1971 on open farmland, the 165-hectare tract is now a densely planted complex of woodlands, wetlands, interpretive gardens and botanical collections. Its well-maintained trails are open to the public and parking is available on site. Interpretive resources include an online guide that allows you to locate any one of more than 2,000 kinds of trees or shrubs now growing there. Access the guide at guelph.arboretumexplorer.org.

GOURMET GUELPH

A visitor can't go wrong at the **Boathouse Tearoom**, located beside the river in parkland next to the Gordon Street bridge. Nowhere else can you partake of high tea served in the most proper fashion and then promptly explore the river in a canoe or kayak rented from **Speed River Paddling**, which is located on the same site. You can rent boats between Victoria Day and Labour Day, and they only accept cash.

Next to the Bookshelf on Quebec Street, **Miijidaa Café + Bistro** takes its name from the Ojibway word meaning "let's eat." It serves a creative mélange of Canadian-rooted cuisine that is consistently well reviewed by visitors. For menus and more, visit miijidaa.ca.

Festivals

♦ Hillside Festival

The flame of hippiedom burns bright just north of Guelph every summer when the annual Hillside Festival takes place. Founded in 1984 with a vision to "create a more vibrant and caring world by promoting altruism, equality, environmentalism and peacemaking in every aspect of its work," the non-profit festival has remained true to its roots while operating a tightly organized weekend of top-flight folk and indie music, crafts, food and political resistance. A winter festival, Hillside Inside, recreates the experience over three days in February, with concerts and spoken-word performances in various spots downtown. See hillsidefestival.ca for all the details.

♦ Eden Mills Writer's Festival

Beginning in a casual fashion with the launch of a new novel by local resident Leon Rooke in 1989, the Eden Mills Writers' Festival is now one of the most established literary events in the province, holding a coveted calendar spot — the first Sunday after Labour Day — in the heart of the publishing season. This ensures the attendance of top-tier talent, including nominees for all the major prizes. The festival is also reliably bucolic, with most of the readings and workshops held outdoors in and around the pretty village of Eden Mills on the Eramosa River. The workshops often sell out, so book early if you want to attend. For more info, see edenmillswritersfestival.ca.

Hillside Festival revellers enjoy the musical acts.

LEFT
Camping sites for the weekend are available, but organizers recommend you book well in advance.

LITERARY SCENE

Guelph has a lively local culture, and its beating heart is the **Bookshelf**, one of the last and best of the country's independent bookstores. It is also one of the most consistently innovative, having added a café in 1980 and a cinema above the bookstore shortly after. Bookshelf.ca was Canada's first full-service online bookstore, and its eBar has hosted a number of famous musicians. But the heart of the operation is still one of the largest stocks of new books you will find on any downtown corner in Canada.

There's a real risk of falling in love with the Donkey's Sanctuary's equine residents.

The Donkey Sanctuary

There's no better way to say it: the Donkey Sanctuary in Aberfoyle, a few kilometres south of Guelph, is having its moment, attracting impressive numbers of urban tourists eager to experience the pleasure of mingling with a large "drove" of these charming animals. There are almost 100 rescued donkeys, mules and hinnies roaming this 40-hectare farm, and even more of them are boarded at foster farms throughout the region. As it grows into a tourist magnet, the sanctuary has expanded its programming with Donkey Talks, an interpretive trail and a learning centre with interactive displays. It's open for visitors on Sundays from May to October and also on Wednesdays during July and August. It's located on Concession Road 4, just west of Highway 6, a few kilometres north of the 401.

WEST

Walk on the wild side at

African Lion Safari

& GALT

The feature that made African Lion Safari unique when it first opened continues to draw legions of zoo-lovers more than 50 years later. Here, it's the people who are enclosed in their vehicles, while the animals are free to roam over hundreds of hectares and seven distinct Game Reserves. There are more than 1,000 species of birds and animals to view, as well as a myriad of attractions geared to keeping families happy.

Endangered Rangers

The superiority of the set-up is reflected in the success of the park's breeding program, which has earned an international reputation for its work with endangered megafauna. Eighteen

All of the other attractions in the park, which have multiplied considerably over the years and now include a boat cruise, train ride and waterpark, are included in the admission price.

elephants have been born here, and the current herd of 16 is the largest in North America. The park has also bred 25 endangered Rothschild's giraffes, of which there are only a few hundred left in the wild, and a remarkable 40 cheetahs. Its herd of five white rhinoceroses is the current focus of a breeding program done in partnership with the Institute of Zoo Biology in Berlin.

The elephants are the biggest stars, performing three times daily in their own arena and going all together for twice-daily swims in a pond. (The

Driving through the Game Reserves gets you close to the animals like never before.

park advises checking its schedule at lionsafari.com and arriving early to get a good view of the swim.) Other sit-down venues are devoted to birds of prey and parrots.

Safari Tour Bus

The most commonly offered advice for visitors here is to pay an extra $5 over the general admission price to ride the park's Safari Tour Bus through the Game Reserves. Driving your own vehicle, as much fun as it may seem, risks damage at the hands of simian vandals, whose rights to scratch, urinate and destroy are thoroughly protected in the fine print of the park's admission policy.

Downtown Galt

Although its address says Hamilton, African Lion Safari is actually closer to the city of Cambridge, a heavy swath of suburban sprawl that enmeshes the old water-powered industrial towns of Galt, Preston and Hespeler. Straddling both banks of the Grand River, downtown Galt best preserves a sense of what it once looked like, and it also has the best selection of lunch spots nearby.

The town was once a major centre of the textile industry, the slow death of which left its historic downtown looking forlorn and shabby despite its scenic location and abundance of historic architecture. The turnaround

began in 2004, with the success of an inspired local campaign to attract University of Waterloo's School of Architecture to Galt. Occupying what was once the Riverside Silk Mill, Waterloo Architecture brought 400 students and staff to town and helped to spark an overdue wave of gentrification.

If you're looking for a sandwich, you can't go wrong at EVO Kitchen, a catering enterprise turned restaurant in the handsome former headquarters of the Galt Knitting Company at 31 Water Street South. Monigram Coffee Roasters at 16 Ainslie Street South, regularly lauded as the best source of java in the region, likewise epitomizes Galt's new vibe.

While exploring the city, don't miss the former Galt Post Office and clock tower, a stunning blend of architectural styles and a National Historic Site. Also be sure to check out the Cambridge Main Street Bridge. It is one of four heritage concrete bowstring arch bridges that span the Grand River (and it can be seen in the 2017 television adaptation of Margaret Atwood's *The Handmaid's Tale*).

A view of the Cambridge Main Street Bridge from along the Grand River.

If you have time while you are in Galt, stop by **McDougall Cottage**, an 1858 granite and limestone labourer's home that celebrates the area's strong Scottish heritage. What makes it special are its hand-painted friezes and *trompe l'oeil* ceilings.

Escape to Paris

A number of local outfitters make exploring the Grand River easy.

Paris is the epitome of the old, handsome valley towns in southern Ontario that have managed to escape the worst ravages of modernism. It seems more like a full-scale diorama of a perfect little place than the real town it actually is. Paris is not only interesting in and of itself, renowned for its distinctive cobblestone buildings, it's also the perfect jumping-off point for a lazy summer float down the bucolic Grand River.

A Grand River Float

The river here is wider than it is upstream at Elora, so it is able to

accommodate all manner of canoes, kayaks, tubes and rafts. From Paris it follows a winding green valley about a dozen kilometres downstream to the Brant Conservation Area on the outskirts of Brantford. It's mostly flat, with a steady current and a few riffles, about as safe as you can get on a river and perfect for those new to paddling.

Local outfitters make it an even easier excursion. The Grand River Rafting Company (grandriverrafting.ca) can supply just about anything that floats — canoes, kayaks, rafts, tubes, stand-up paddleboards — for daily rent or as part of a guided tour. Cross-town competitor Grand Experiences (grand-experiences.com) offers a similar menu. In addition to floats down the Grand, both companies lead some more adventurous tours in the region, including overnight camping trips and moonlit paddles.

A Scenic Bicycle Shuttle

One advantage of renting is that the outfitters will shuttle you back to your car at the end of the trip. However, this is an ideal opportunity to arrange your own shuttle, simply by dropping off a bicycle (or two) at the takeout point in Brantford before you start and riding back to Paris when you finish. The ride back is almost entirely off-road, following the Oak Hill Trail from the conservation area, crossing a bridge to the east side of the river and picking up the S.C. Johnson Trail back to Paris.

The **Cambridge to Paris Rail Trail** is 18 kilometres of level, fine-gravel recreational trail through the forests along the Grand River — a lovely path for hikers and an easy round trip for cyclists.

A view of charming Paris.

The curved cobblestone facade of 7 Burwell Street in Paris.

For more on cobblestone houses in Paris, including a comprehensive list and images, visit canadacobblestone. blogspot.ca.

(such as the curved-facade dispensary at 7 Burwell Street) and unique (like the Greek-influenced home at 16 Broadway Street) to the truly grand (such as stately Hamilton Place at 165 Grand River Street North). Another fine cobblestone house worth seeing is Alexander Graham Bell's first address in Canada, located at 22 Church Street.

The Paris Museum & Historical Society offers guided tours and also publishes a self-guided walking tour. Maps are available at the Arlington Hotel, an architectural destination in its own right (and a place to dine), located at 106 Grand River Street North. The self-guided tour, which takes under an hour to complete, is well worth the time.

The trail overlooks the Grand River and travels through farm fields and rare prairie grasslands. Like the float down, the ride back is about a dozen kilometres, and together they add up to a full day's activity.

Cobblestone Houses of Paris

None of that leaves much time for Paris, which more than deserves a look over. The town is best known for a collection of houses built of immaculately arranged cobblestones, a technique imported from New York State by builder Levi Boughton. They range from the beautifully simple

For something sweet, head to **Chocolate Sensations**. Delicious homemade treats include fudge, sponge toffee and peanut butter cups. They also carry pop, lemonade and Kawartha Dairy ice cream.

Dining

If it were located anywhere closer to Toronto, a window table at Stillwaters Plate and Pour would be harder to get than a seat on the Yonge line at rush hour. Located in the centre of a red-brick row of commercial buildings facing Grand River Street on one side and the river lapping their foundations in the rear, the restaurant opens to the water with a large, airy dining room, a couple of riverside patios and a rooftop patio as well. You can reserve a window seat during the off-season, but there are no guarantees when the weather turns warm.

The tempting riverside patios of Stillwaters restaurant.

Located in a restored historic wool mill dating from 1889, the **Paris Wincey Mills Co.** on Mechanic Street is a vibrant year-round indoor market with a range of vendors and a café. This great community spot is open Thursdays, Fridays and Saturdays.

"RETAIL-TAINMENT" AT PARIS SURF

You could fly to Los Angeles to discover the latest beachwear and food trends, or you could drive to Paris, Ontario, home of one of the most original and entertaining retail and food experiences you will ever find. The brainchild of California blue jeans magnate Chip Foster, one half of design duo Chip and Pepper, **Paris Surf** was created to prototype an entirely new brand and, ultimately, chain of stores. "Walk in and you're in Venice Beach," Foster told the *Toronto Star*. "The environment is *sick*. We didn't hold out on *anything*."

The bright and lively space is crammed with trucker hats, baggy sweats and jeans, with a wood-fired pizza oven and restaurant in the back. Neither this nor any other Paris has ever seen anything like it. You'll find Paris Surf downtown on Mechanic Street.

Visit Six Nations
OF THE GRAND RIVER

The Six Nations of the Grand River is the most historic of the old "Indian reserves" in Ontario — indeed the very first — ceded by the British to followers of war chief Thayendanegea (Joseph Brant) after the loss of the original Haudenosaunee homeland during the Revolutionary War. Today it's an inspiring example of cultural continuity despite every challenge and a fascinating place to visit. "We're still here," the Six Nations tourist office reminds us. "And we invite you to come and find us."

The six nations that make up the people of Six Nations are Mohawk, Cayuga, Onondaga, Oneida, Tuscarora and Seneca.

July Powwow on the Grand

The most popular tourist event here is the Grand River Powwow, held every summer on the last weekend in July, which draws 400 dancers in full regalia for a celebration of Indigenous culture. Built around a series of competitive dances, it's an incredibly colourful event, highly photogenic, with bleacher seating available for those who arrive early. There is also a market with nearly 100 vendors selling a huge variety

of Indigenous food and crafts. See grpowwow.ca for more information about getting there (it's complicated) and event etiquette.

Year-Round Day Tours

For visiting at other times of year, the community has developed three packaged day tours that make it easy. One tour focuses on the history and culture of the Grand River settlement, another on the arts and the third is a sports tour that includes instruction in lacrosse from the people who invented the game. See sixnationstourism.ca for details.

If you intend to tour on your own, in-depth guidance is easily available at the tourist office, which you will find on County Road 54 at Chiefswood

Road, midway between Brantford and Caledonia.

Historic Sites

Six Nations covers a large territory and there's much to see and do, including Kanata Village, with its full scale wooden longhouse, and Kayanase, a greenhouse dedicated to preserving and propagating Indigenous seeds. You can even play bingo or watch a lacrosse game on the weekends. However, the three monuments to Six Nations history on the following pages are not to be missed.

More shopping opportunities are available in November during the holiday craft fairs.

Dancers in full regalia at the annual Grand River Powwow.

◆ Chiefswood National Historic Site

The Chiefswood National Historic Site, where the powwow takes place, centres on the historic mansion where the Mohawk poet Pauline Johnson was born in 1861. It has two front doors: one to greet Indigenous people arriving by canoe from the river, and another to greet visitors travelling by road, a practical accommodation with rich symbolic meaning for First Nations Loyalists. Their descendants have big plans for the site, including the introduction of a "glamping" facility by the riverside. For the time being, there are tours of the building available throughout the summer. Find Chiefswood at 1037 Highway 54 and Chiefswood Road in Ohsweken.

◆ Her Majesty's Royal Chapel of the Mohawks

Built in 1785, Her Majesty's Royal Chapel of the Mohawks is the oldest church in Ontario and one of only two in the country officially designated "royal." It is the last remnant of what was once Brant's Mohawk village, which was forcibly removed in the 19th century to make way for the burgeoning industrial city of Brantford. Although simple and much altered over the centuries, it is still important enough to have been visited by Queen Elizabeth II.

The chapel is open for guided tours every day but Mondays from Victoria Day long weekend to Thanksgiving weekend, but note that you need to obtain written permission to photograph the interior and its unique stained glass windows.

✦ Woodland Cultural Centre

Just down the road is the Woodland Cultural Centre, a monument to Indigenous resilience housed in the former building of the notorious Mohawk Institute Indian Residential School, where generations of children were virtually imprisoned in the name of education over 150 years. It is now undergoing a thorough renovation. In the meantime, the centre remains a thriving community hub, with a museum that draws on the largest collection of artifacts in First Nations' hands. It's an excellent introduction to the history of the Six Nations — told from their point of view. The centre also includes a library and an art gallery, which has mounted a juried First Nations art exhibition annually since 1975. See woodlandculturalcentre.ca for more information.

Arts and Crafts Shopping

There is an abundance of stores and galleries within the Six Nations' borders, producing traditional pottery, beadwork, clothing and contemporary art. Finding them, however, can be its own adventure. The answer is to begin at the tourist office near Chiefswood and get a map. Be sure to check out the following places:

• The original and largest craft shop at Six Nations is Iroqrafts, located just east of the village of Ohsweken on Tuscarora Road. The smell of sweetgrass and deerskin greets visitors. In addition to artwork and gift items, Iroqrafts also supplies a large selection of beads and supplies for crafters.

• You can find another good selection of Indigenous artwork at I&S Crafts and Supplies, located on Third Line at Cayuga Road.

• Artist Traccy Anthony expresses his heritage with a distinctive punk sensibility in the art and apparel he sells at Vision Artworks, which is located in the New Credit Plaza on Highway 6, just outside of Hagersville.

And if the sin of smoking still besets you, you'll find a high-class den of tax-free iniquity, including a fine selection of Cuban cigars, at the Cigar and Pipe Emporium in the same plaza.

BURGERS AND MORE

Those seeking full immersion into the cultural life of the famous Six Nations shouldn't miss a visit to the **Burger Barn**, a justly celebrated local institution that draws custom from throughout the county and beyond. It's large and loud, with food that's cheap and tasty. The combination is sufficiently popular you will often encounter lineups for lunch, especially on weekends. You can find the Burger Barn on the Fourth Line directly east of Ohsweken.

If the crowd's too much for you, the **Argyle St. Grill** at 345 Argyle Street South in the nearby town of Caledonia serves similar fare in a quieter setting.

WEST

Fall for Elora

Is there one single best weekend day trip out of Toronto? Given the diversity of both individual interests and the opportunities at hand, the question almost seems silly. But in fact there is an answer, and its name is Elora.

In a world where every crossroads strives for some small distinction, Elora confidently proclaims itself "Ontario's most beautiful village." And it's true: Walt Disney himself couldn't have improved on this perfectly ordered jumble of Victorian quaintness, dramatically straddling the entrance to the deepest gorge of the 300-kilometre-long Grand River. It was here that painter A.J. Casson, celebrated for his warm scenes of old Ontario, found his greatest inspiration — as have generations of calendar and postcard makers ever since, reliably entranced by Elora's old stone mills and tumbling falls.

The fact that Elora does so closely resemble a high-class theme park could conceivably, someday, work against it. More intensive development is underway and preciousness approaches, but in the meantime it's a jewel.

The attraction of the village is not merely its setting and shops, all of

which are pitched to visitors. The Elora Gorge is worth a trip, proving the easily accessible antithesis to the town's more commercial propositions. Yin and yang combine effortlessly to make a full day here.

Downtown Shopping and Dining

Elora is choked with galleries, boutiques, cafés and restaurants, many catering to a sophisticated urban clientele. More will come soon when the 1833 Elora Mill reopens after a long renovation and its developers connect it, by means of a glass bridge over the Grand, to a new mixed-use project on the south bank of the river. For maximum shopping, visit Elora on a Saturday morning and begin your tour at the Elora Farmer's Market, located at the edge of town beside the Grand River Raceway.

These are just a few of the dining and shopping highlights to be discovered:

- Desert Rose Café offers tasty vegetarian fare in a quaint storefront.
- The Shepherd's Pub has pub classics in cozy comfort overlooking the river.
- Blown Away Glass Studio is your go-to for beautiful hand-blown glass. You can also watch the artists at work from inside the gallery.

The village of Elora is pretty enough for a postcard.

An atmospheric section of the Elora Gorge Trail.

Exploring the Gorge

The spectacular 22-metre-high limestone cliffs and rushing waters of Elora Gorge are one of the most beautiful sights of the Grand River Valley. You don't want to visit Elora without at least taking a peek. And there's something for everyone who wants to explore it.

◆ Hiking the Elora Gorge Trail

Bring your hiking boots and jump right in. The Elora Gorge Trail traces both banks of the river downstream from the

village, with lookouts making the most of the dramatic scenery. Campgrounds populate the north shore, which can make it crowded. The main trail on the south side cuts through the day-use area of the Elora Gorge Conservation Area. You can get to it on foot from the village, but construction sites and fences make the trailhead hard to find. The conservation authority wants you to drive west on County Road 21 and enter through its gatehouse, where you will also find ample parking and washroom facilities.

HIKING OR CYCLING THE ELORA CATARACT TRAILWAY

The **Elora Cataract Trailway** is a well-maintained scenic rail trail that runs 47 kilometres east of the village to Cataract Road in the **Forks of the Credit Provincial Park**, crossing the height of land that separates the Grand and Credit watersheds. The trailway, which is ideal for hiking or biking, passes through the handsome valley town of **Fergus** a few kilometres upstream from Elora. It also skirts the **Bellwood Lake Conservation Area,** a lovely spot for a swim or picnic. Keep in mind that this is first-class trout water, thanks to an ambitious program that has seen the Grand stocked with more than 20,000 trout fry every year for the past two decades. **Grand River Troutfitters** (grandrivertroutfitters.com) in Fergus can help you catch some.

• Zipping, Climbing and Rappelling

If you can't be bothered to visit the gorge on foot, you can always fly over it on the Elora SkyRider Zipline. Local adventure company One Axe Pursuits (oneaxepursuits.com) offers single rides and daily passes as well as more advanced courses in zipping, climbing and rappelling on the steep limestone cliffs of the gorge.

• Tubing the Rapids

The spring flood brings expert white-water rafters to paddle the challenging rapids of the gorge, but summer is for tubing. It's now the park's most popular activity. The ride is 2 kilometres long, passing under closely spaced cliffs that soar above the river. Permits and equipment rentals are available at the park gatehouse. A shuttle bus operates on weekends to carry tubers back upstream. The operation shuts down during high-water conditions, so before packing your swimsuits make sure to check with the park at 519-846-9742.

Tubing along the Grand River in Elora.

Summer music festival lovers can't do much better than Elora's **Riverfest**, which takes place over an August weekend in Bissell Park.

CANOEING TO THE WEST MONTROSE COVERED BRIDGE

For those willing to venture farther downriver and organize a shuttle, the canoe route from Elora to **West Montrose** is a leisurely half-day float. A visit to the picturesque **West Montrose Covered Bridge** — the only one of its type remaining in Ontario — is worthwhile no matter how you get there. To get there by car or bike from Elora, follow Middlebrook Road 12 kilometres south of Elora until you meet the river. (See page 232 for more information about the bridge.)

Shop in St. Jacobs

In the early 19th century, Old Order Mennonites from Pennsylvania purchased the land that became St. Jacobs sometime after Mohawk chief Joseph Brant (Thayendanegea) sold the land in blocks to speculators to raise money for the Six Nations. The village began to grow when a dam on the Conestogo River was built to provide water power for saw and woollen mills. St. Jacobs still maintains a large and visible Mennonite presence, which is part of its attraction as a thriving tourist destination.

St. Jacobs Farmers' Market

The village of St. Jacobs was just a dot on the map until 1975, when an enterprising group of local farmers erected tents on a former stockyard outside the village and called it the St. Jacobs Farmers' Market. It was one of the first of its kind, and today it is the largest farmers' market in the country, drawing one million visitors every year. Fresh food from local fields is barely half the story in this sprawling emporium, where hundreds of vendors offer every kind of art, craft and knick-knack, from tin ceiling tiles to heraldic

coasters. The market fills several buildings and straggles over the pavements, like a feral Walmart. The opening of an actual Walmart next door, along with the expansion of prosperous Waterloo to the south, has transformed the scene from rural to suburban over the years, but it's still a phenomenon.

Shopping the Village

Like nearby Elora (pages 224–7), St. Jacobs entered the heritage game early, and the village is now packed with shops and studios peddling artisanal wares of every description. A detailed account of all the shops and restaurants

in the village and the farmers' market is available at stjacobs.com. Suffice it to say that there are more than enough vendors here to fill a regional mall, and if that's what St. Jacobs feels like on a busy summer Saturday, such is the price of success.

Artefacts Salvage and Design is a truly unique shop that's always worth a browse for treasures you never knew

The farmers' market is a bustling destination during the summer.

The market is open twice a week, on Thursdays and Saturdays year round, plus Tuesdays in the summer.

Shopping is plentiful in St. Jacob's village.

you needed, from beautiful stained glass windows to classical columns or floor tiles salvaged from a Cairo café. It's located on Isabella, the western-most north-south street in the village, at No. 46.

Ten Thousand Villages is the local branch of a retail chain dedicated to creating opportunities for artisans in developing countries. The shop is located on King Street, which is the main drag.

Mennonite Country

Surrounded by Mennonite farms on the rich soil of Waterloo County, St. Jacobs has become a showcase where the modern world can peer into the mysterious Old Order. You can learn a lot chatting with the Mennonite farmers at the market, or you can go deeper…

If you haven't eaten your fill at the farmers' market, the **Stone Crock** restaurant on King Street in the village is a popular spot for lunch, so much so that you might have to wait for a table on summer weekends. If you're serious about coffee, **EcoCafe Village Roasters**, also on King Street, is probably the most serious coffee shop you're likely to find west of Toronto.

◆ Mennonite Story Interpretative Centre

Visit the Mennonite Story Interpretative Centre, where you can learn about the local and global (1.5 million members) Mennonite community and step into a replica Old Order meeting house. The volunteer-run centre is on King Street North, next to the post office. Admission is by donation.

• St. Jacobs Horse-Drawn Tours

Consider making time for a farm visit with St. Jacobs Horse-Drawn Tours (stjacobshorsedrawntours.com), which gives tourists a glimpse of Mennonite life from within a converted San Francisco trolley drawn by two enormous draft horses. The farm tour takes an hour and 15 minutes, and tickets are available at the south end of the main farmers' market next to the Quilted Heirlooms log cabin. The same company also offers buggy rides and genuine sleigh rides in the winter.

• Heritage Rail

For full immersion in obsolete modes of transportation, the Waterloo Central Railway (waterloocentralrailway.com) runs trips between the farmers' market and the village of Elmira on a regular schedule every market day. The best trips take place on long weekends, when the volunteers who operate this non-profit branch line hook a fire-breathing steam locomotive to the front of the train. For true rail geeks, the St. Jacobs & Aberfoyle Model Railway, "North America's finest 'O'

Scale Layout," depicts southern Ontario as it appeared in the 1950s. The model is located on King Street North, just south of the bridge over the Conestogo River, and is open weekends only.

Horse-drawn buggies are common sights in and around St. Jacobs

MAPLE SYRUP MANIA

A 10-minute drive north from St. Jacobs, the village of Elmira hosts the **Elmira Maple Syrup Festival** every spring — the world's largest single-day maple syrup festival, according to Guinness World Records. Come for the pancakes, apple fritters, homemade toffee, log-sawing competitions, Mennonite quilts and other crafts, sugar bush tours and…maple syrup, of course. Visit elmiramaplesyrup.com for more details.

The unique West Montrose Covered Bridge.

West Montrose Covered Bridge

If St. Jacobs is beginning to feel too suburban, one need only drive 10 minutes north to enter the most picturesque rural scene in Ontario: the banks of the Grand River where it is crossed by the West Montrose Covered Bridge, also known as the Kissing Bridge, built in 1881 and now the last of its type in the province. It is so picturesque that the area is dotted with signs demanding fees from photographers who want to shoot the bridge from the best locations, which are all on private property. But there is a public parking lot and small picnic area off Letson Road on the south bank of the river, just east of the bridge. To get there from St. Jacobs, follow King Street north of the river to Sawmill Road (Regional Road 17), travel east 1 kilometre to Northfield Drive (Road 22), north 5 kilometres to Hill Street and east again to West Montrose.

While you are stepping back in history, why not look for some time-worn treasures? Next door to the farmers' market, you'll find the **St. Jacobs Antiques Market**, and a five-minute walk down the road on Weber Street takes you to **Market Road Antiques**.

WEST

Take in a show at Stratford

Along with Niagara Falls, no day-trip destination out of Toronto comes closer to compulsory than the Stratford Festival. What sets Stratford apart is that it's worth visiting every year, offering an ever-changing repertoire of consistently high-quality theatrical productions. (Once predominantly Shakespearean, the repertoire is now much more eclectic.) Like Niagara, it's a miracle we're apt to take for granted, or even to overlook as the ever-growing city scene dominates our attention. For some, Stratford is too stuffy. For others, it's too commercial. But in any view, it's unique — and a treasure for all those who still value the classical repertoire.

Stratford is also the best-organized and most accessible big event on the cultural calendar, a result of 60 years' experience enticing tourists from hundreds of kilometres away on both sides of the border. Everything works smoothly, from ticketing to picnicking, and all the guidance you really need is available at stratfordfestival.ca.

Shakespearean Gardens contains 60 plant species mentioned in Shakespeare's plays.

Going the Distance

The drive to get there and back is longer than most in this book, which is why so many visitors opt to stay overnight. However, you can also get there and back in a day quite comfortably on public transit.

If you want to ride the rails, VIA Rail train No. 85 leaves Union Station most days at 10:55 a.m., arriving in Stratford in time for a quick lunch before a 2 p.m. matinee. You also have time for a post-show dinner before boarding train No. 88, which leaves Stratford for Toronto at 9:05 p.m.

The best deal in this book is probably the festival's own Stratford Direct Bus, which at press time cost $29 for a round trip from downtown Toronto.

The schedule is flexible, with late-night returns that allow for dinners and evening shows as well as matinees. The buses leave at 10 a.m. from the Intercontinental Hotel on Front Street, just west of Union Station, and pick up returning passengers at all four theatres in Stratford. You need to reserve a seat in advance and to have already bought theatre tickets to board.

If you do decide to go the distance by car, be warned that parking can be a real challenge in Stratford, especially around the downtown theatres. You can reserve a space in advance at the Festival Theatre by calling the box office at 1-800-567-1600.

Getting Your Tickets — Ahead of Time

The beauty of most day trips is that they require little if any advance planning, but that is decidedly not the case with Stratford. By the time you read the glowing review that inspires you to attend the festival in late spring, tickets to the show in question will already be scarce, expensive or even gone. The best time to plan your trip is January, when the festival announces its upcoming program and only the enthusiasts are enthused. You can choose your dates and take advantage of any number of deals and discounts offered on the festival website.

One advantage of waiting, of course, is that you can heed the chirping of the crickets before making your choice of what to see. Every reviewer still in the business offers opinions about the full season, and their efforts are helpfully compiled at stratfordfestivalreviews.com.

Festival Theatre began in 1953 as a tent erected over a wooden stage.

BEHIND-THE-SCENES DIVERSIONS

The festival's **Costume and Props Warehouse** in downtown Stratford rivals the smaller theatres for its popularity among visitors. It's a fabulous smorgasbord of theatrical magic, and don't forget to snap a picture of you or your loved ones in costume at the end of the tour. The festival also offers tours of its archives, gardens and the **Stratford Perth Museum**. See stratfordfestival.ca for schedules and tickets.

Culinary Destinations

Forty years of white-linen tradition came to an end with the closure of Rundles, the restaurant that pioneered Stratford's now-thriving culinary scene. With it has gone the expectation that dining here must be a formal affair — either that or pizza. The town now has such a great variety of casual, on-trend restaurants that it merits the status of a culinary destination in its own right, worth visiting even when the theatres are closed. The farm-to-table movement is especially strong here, led by the Stratford Chefs League, "a group of chefs uniting farms, restaurants and each other through food," and nourished by the rich farmlands of surrounding Perth County. Here are a few standout options:

• Located at 64 Wellington Street, Red Rabbit typifies the new breed of Stratford restaurant. Opened by veterans of the Church — another defunct white-linen restaurant, since transformed into the popular Revival House — the Red Rabbit is a worker-owned enterprise that specializes in locally grown food.

• A few doors down the street, Monforte on Wellington serves a menu based on the cheese produced by the local dairy of the same name. It's owned by Ruth Klahsen, founder of the Stratford Chefs School at 136 Ontario Street, which serves prix fixe dinners to the public in fall and winter only.

• Just around the corner at 37 Market Place, the Revel Caffe is a favourite of locals and actors.

• Among the fine-dining restaurants that will require reservations, standouts include the Prune at 151 Albert Street, Bijou at 105 Erie Street and the Restaurant at the Bruce on Parkview Drive at King Street.

One thing that hasn't changed in Stratford is the seating schedule, which works around curtain times with pre-theatre and post-theatre seatings. Visitstratford.ca maintains well-organized listings that make choosing one out of the dozens of restaurants easier.

No time to dine? Light lunches, beverages and snacks are available at the Festival Theatre. Snacks and beverages are also available at the other theatres. You can even order a picnic lunch straight from the Festival Threatre box office at 1-800-567-1600 and enjoy the pretty park-like riverside setting nearby.

Photo Credits

Alamy
  Bill Brooks: 140, 146 (top);
  Gaertner: 24
Alana Lee Photography: 152 (top),
  153 (bottom)
Andrea Hamlin: 57 (top)
Art Gallery of Hamilton: 75
Bloomfield Bicycle Company: 186
Canadian Automotive Museum: 134
  (top)
The Canadian Canoe Museum: 171
Chris May: 65
Conservation Halton: 205 (left), 206
  (bottom)
Cori Arthur: 169
Courtesy of Library of Congress,
  LC-DIG-ppmsca-54230: 124
David Bree: 180 (bottom)
Elizabeth Aikenhead: 168
Eric Dumigan: 201, 202 (top)
Gallery on the Farm: 150
Garry Kan: 56
Hardwood Ski and Bike: 68 (right)
iStock
  buzbuzzer: 95 (top);
  JonathanNicholls: 92 (top);
  lishanskyphotography: 54 (right);
  modesigns58: 90, 209 (bottom),
  210; Orchidpoet: 59, 172 (bottom)
Jack Tome: 22
Jean Simard: 157 (left)
Jennifer Copeland: 69 (top)
John Barber: 7, 16 (left), 25, 26, 38, 39,
  48 (top), 76, 88 (left), 91, 100, 105
  (right), 112, 120 (left), 123, 135, 136,
  149 (bottom), 157 (right), 158, 161,
  173 (right), 174, 176, 177, 187 (top),
  192 (bottom), 219 (bottom), 222
John R. Walker: 148, 149 (top)
Kerry Jarvis: 45 (top)
Kristie Woods: 58 (top), 61, 62, 63
  (right)
Logan Brazeau: 154
Long Point Eco Adventures: 121
  (bottom)
Nature Conservancy of Canada: 19, 21
Nhl4hamilton/Wikimedia Commons:
  78 (right), 80
Niagara Parks: 98, 99, 103, 104, 105
  (left), 106,
Norfolktourism.ca: 119, 120 (right),
  121 (top), 122 (top)
Northumberland Tourism/Richard J.
  Kettle: 159, 165, 167, 179 (top)

Northumberland Tourism/Ted
  Amsden: 180 (top), 181
Nottawasaga Valley Conservation
  Authority: 36, 37 (bottom)
Ontario Tourism Marketing
  Partnership Corporation: 15, 16
  (right), 28, 33, 47, 58 (bottom), 68
  (left), 101, 102, 107, 108, 109, 134
  (bottom), 160, 182, 184 (top), 204,
  205 (right), 206 (top), 211, 214, 216,
  221, 227, 230, 231 (top), 235
Philip Jackman: 42 (bottom), 43, 44
Robert McLaughlin Gallery/Michal
  Cullen: 132, 133
Sarah Tacoma: 64
Shutterstock
  Alastair Wallace: 82, 185; Alexander
  Sviridov: 83 (right); Alexandra
  Lande: 202 (bottom); Angelo
  Cordeschi: 55; AnjelikaGr: 110, 209
  (top); Anna Mente: 50 (bottom);
  Ari N: 223; asobov: 212; BORODIN
  DENIS: 52 (bottom); canoak: 188;
  Claudiu Dobre: 30, 37 (top); Dan
  Elias: 92 (bottom); Darlene Munro:
  83 (left); DCWPhoto: 144 (top);
  Edward Fielding: 207 (bottom);
  emkaplin: 81 (bottom); FamVeld:
  138 ; Fribus Mara: 123–5 (trees);
  Gary Blakeley: 184 (bottom);
  Greens87: 1; Gus Garcia: 145;
  Harold Stiver: 215; Images by
  Maria: 95 (bottom); IVY PHOTOS:
  234; JamesJongPhotography: 84;
  JHVEPhoto: 94 (bottom), 163, 218,
  219 (top), 229; John Fader: 172
  (top); JPDworld: 31 (top); Justin
  Atkins: 122 (bottom); Karina Elise
  Designs: 42 (top); Ken Felepchuk:
  115; LaiQuocAnh: 35; LesPalenik:
  41, 117; LovArt: 123 (star), 125
  (star); marevos imaging: 85 (left);
  Marc Filion: 226 (bottom); Margoe
  Edwards: 231 (bottom); Mark Evers
  Photography: 49, 66 (bottom);
  Mascha Tace: 8, 70, 126, 194; Matt
  Ledwinka: 50 (bottom); mikecphoto:
  97; Mishy Laine: 226 (top); Monkey
  Business Images: 31 (bottom),
  57 (bottom); Norman Pogson:
  63 (left); Olesya Baron: 94 (top);
  ornavi: 191–3 (background); Patrick
  Messier: 48 (bottom); Paul Reeves
  Photography: 54 (left), 146 (bottom);

  PEPPERSMINT: 144 (bottom);
  PGMart: 67–69 (background);
  Philip Lange: 191 (bottom); PitK:
  96; Rick Blaxall: 32; RT Images: 179
  (bottom); SF photo: 85 (right), 217;
  Sharon Rego: 17; ShibaE: 191–3
  (cyclists); Stacey Newman: 207
  (top); StephenRussellSmithPhotos:
  152; studio4pic: 187 (bottom);
  studiolaska: 66 (top); Tom Worsley:
  29, 173 (left), 232; Tony Moran:
  225; Ulga: 20; Vaclav Mach: 190;
  ValeStock: 189; Zolnierek: 45
  (bottom)
Sifton Cook Heritage Centre: 164
Tourism Hamilton: 77, 78 (left), 81
  (top), 87 (bottom), 88 (right), 89,
  193 (top)
Town of Wasaga Beach: 52 (top), 53
Township of Uxbridge & Central
  Counties Tourism: 141, 142
Treetop Trekking Ganaraska: 153
  (top)
Logo vectors (Shutterstock):
  AF studio; Alexander
  Lysenko; andromina; Arcady;
  ARTBALANCE; AVS-Images;
  browndogstudios; cheesekerbs;
  FMStox; graphic stocker; HN
  Works; i3alda; In-finity; Irina
  Adamovich; Janis Abolins;
  KASUE; LynxVector; Martial Red;
  musmellow; Nadin3d; Nikolai
  Petrovich; n o o m; notbad;
  Powerful Design; Rashad Ashurov;
  RedKoala; Sergey Furtaev;
  SVIATLANA SHEINA; uchenik;
  vectorchef; vectorEps; VoodooDot;
  Webicon

FRONT COVER
Top left: Andrea Hamlin
Top middle: Niagara Parks
Top right: Shutterstock/Tony Moran
Skyline: Shutterstock/Greens87
Car: Shutterstock/Mascha Tace
Road: Shutterstock/fluidworkshop

BACK COVER
Top: Tourism Hamilton
Bottom: Ontario Tourism Marketing
  Partnership Corporation
Skyline: Shutterstock/Greens87

Index

Page numbers in italics represent photos.

African Lion Safari, 213–14, *214*
airplanes, 86–7, 200–2
Albion Falls, 85, *85*
Albion Hills Conservation Area, 17, *17*
Alton, 33
Annina's Bakeshop, 138
apples, 63, 207
Arboretum (Guelph), 210
Arboretum (RBG), 81
art, 14–16, 42–3, 65, 74–7, 105, 132–4, 205, 223, 225
art crawls, 76–7, *77*
Art Gallery of Hamilton (AGH), 75–6, *75*

Backus Woods, 122, *122*
Baldwin, Robert, 24–5
Barnum House, 167, *167*
Barrie, 36–8
Barton Trail Route, 142
Basilica of Our Lady Immaculate, 208–9, *209*
beaches, 51–4, 119, 162–3, 181, 188
Beaver Valley, 66
Belfountain, 29–30
Belfountain Conservation Area, 30, *30*
Bertie Hall mansion, 125
Betty's Pies and Tarts, 161
Bicycle Café, 64, *64*
Binder Twine Festival, 16
bird watching, 120–2, 178–80
Black Robe (film), 47
Bloomfield Bicycle Company, 186, *186*, 188–9
Blue Mountain Village, 55–9, *56–7*
Bookshelf bookstore, 212
Boyne Valley Provincial Park, 35
Brampton, 202
Brighton, 181
Brighton Speedway, 181, *181*

Brock monument, *102*, 103
Bruce Trail, 29, 35, 59, 84
Burger Barn, 223
Burke House, *112*
Burlington, 193
bus tours, 94, 95–6
Butler's Barracks, 116
butter tarts, 41–2, *42*
Butterfly Conservatory, 100

Caledon Hills, 31
Cambridge Main Street Bridge, 215, *215*
Cambridge to Paris Rail Trail, 217
Camp 30, 155
Canadian Automotive Museum, 134, *134*
Canadian Canoe Museum, 170–1, *171*
Canadian Tire Motorsport Park, 147–9, *148–9*
Canadian Warplane Heritage Museum, 86–7, *87*
canoeing, 37, 216–17, 227
Capitol Theatre, 160, *160*
cars, 134, 147–9, 181
Casino Rama, 45
caves, 174
Cheltenham, 33
Chiefswood National Historic Site, 222
Chocolate Sensations, 218
Chudleigh's, 207
churches, 115, 123–4, 127, 157, 159
climbing, 227
cobblestone houses, 218
Cobourg, 162–5
Cobourg Beach, 162–3, *163*
Collingwood, 55–9
Cootes Paradise Marsh, 81, *81*
Copeland Forest, 69
Court House Theatre, *114*
Crawford Lake Conservation Area, 204–5, *205*
Credit River Valley, 27–31, 193

Credit Road, *31*
Creemore, 38–9
Creemore Springs Brewery, 38, *39*
Crooks' Hollow, 83–4
The Crossing/Freedom Park, 125
cycling trips, 14–18, 31, 91, 97–101, 111, 120, 139–40, 153–4, 164–5, 173–4, 185–93, 217

Deer Clan Longhouse, 205
Devil's Pulpit, 28
Devil's Punchbowl, 85, *85*
Discovery Harbour, 49–50
Donkey Sanctuary, 212, *212*
Dundas, 82
Dundas Peak, 84
Dundurn Castle, 89

Ebenezer, Doan, *25*, 26
Eden Mills Writers' Festival, 211
Elias Smith House, 159
Elora, 224–7, *225*
Elora Gorge, 226–7
Elora Gorge Trail, 226, *226*
EPIC Trail, 154
Erin, 30
Eugenia Falls, 66

Fallsview Casino, *95*
Festival Theatre (Stratford), *235*, 236
festivals, 16–17, 44–5, 53–4, 114, 116–17, 168, 184, 211, 231, 233–5
Fife, David, 175–6
fishing, 18, *144–5*, 145, 173–4
Fishway, 81–2
Flesherton, 64–5
Flesherton Art Gallery, 65
forests, 69, 122, 135–6, 151–5. *see also* parks and conservation areas
Forks of the Credit Provincial Park, 29, *29*
Forks of the Credit Road, 27–9, *28*
Fort George, 116, *116*
Fort Willow, 37
4th Line Theatre, 177

Gallery on the Farm, 150, *150*
Galt, 214–15
Ganaraska Forest, 151–5, *152–3*
Ganaraska Forest Centre, 152, *152*
gardens, 79–81, 234
gay communities, 168
Geissberger Farmhouse Cider, 150
Georgian Bay, 51–3
Georgian Hills Vineyards, 62
Glen Eden ski hill, 205
Glen Haffy Conservation Area, 18
Glen Major Conservation Area, 135–7, *135*
Glen Major Methodist Church, 137
Glenelg, 65, *65*
GO Niagara Bike Train, 97–8
GO Transit, 191–3
Goldie Feldman Nature, *19*, 20–2
Goodrich-Loomis Conservation Area, 169, *169*
Goodwood, 139–40
Grafton, 167
Grand River, *215–16*, 216–19, *219*, 227
Grand River Powwow, 220–1, *221*
Grandma's Beach Treats, 53
Great Lakes Waterfront Trail, 191–2
Great War Flying Museum, 200–2, *201*
Greenbelt Cycling Route, 193
Guelph, 208–12
Guelph Civic Museum, 209–10, *209*

Halton Parks, 202–7, *204–5*
Hamilton, *76–8*
art and architecture, 74–8
gardens and waterfalls, 79–85
history and heritage, 86–9
Hamilton City Hall, 78
Hamilton Museum of Steam and Technology, 88–9, *88*
Hammond Museum of Radio, 210
Happy Valley Forest, 19–22, *19–22*
Hardwood Ski and Bike, 68
Haute Goat, 161, *161*
the Headwaters, 32–5
Henson, Josiah, 125
Her Majesty's Royal Chapel of the Mohawks, 222
hiking, 18, 19–22, 54, 62, 66, 83–4, 84, 85, 89, 136–7, 142, 153, 217, 226. see also Bruce Trail
Hillside Festival, 211, *211*
Hilton Falls, 206, *206*

historic sites, 46–8, 53, 87–9, 102–6, 116, 123–5, 134, 140, 159, 172, 177, 208–10, 215, 221–2, 232
H.M.S. *Haida* National Historic Site, 88–7, *88*
H.M.S. *Nancy*, 53
H.M.S. *Tecumseth*, 49–50, *50*
Hogg's Falls, 66
Hope Mill, 176, *176*
horseback riding, 33–4, 142, 153
Horseshoe Valley Resort, 68
Humber Valley, 14–18
Humber Valley Heritage Trail, 18

Indian food, 202
Indigenous landmarks, 46–8, 103–4, 116, 204–5, 220–3
Iroqrafts, 223

Johnson, Pauline, 222

Kanata Village, 221
Kelso Conservation Area, 205–6
Kite Festival, 53
Kleinburg, 16
Kolapore Uplands, 60–3, *61*
Kortright Centre for Conservation, 16–17, *16*

LaFontaine, Louis-Hippolyte, 25
Lake Erie, 118–22
Lake Scugog, 143–5, *144–5*
Lakefield, 173–4
Landscape of Nations memorial, 103–4, *103*
Lang Grist Mill, 175, *176*
Lang Pioneer Village and Museum, 175–6
Lang-Hastings rail trail, 177
Laura Secord Homestead, 104, *105*
Laveanne Lavender Farm, *154*, 155
Leacock Museum National Historic Site, 44, *44*
Leaskdale, 140–1
Lesser Niagara Circle Route, 99–101
Lighthouse Interpretive Centre, 180, *180*
Linwood Acres Trout, 155
Lloydtown, 22, *22*
L.M. Montgomery's Leaskdale Manse National Historic Site, 140, *141*
Long Point, 120–2, *121*

Long Point Bay, 122
Luke, Alexandra, 133

Mack, Charles, 30
Mackenzie Printery, 105–6, *105*
maple syrup festivals, 16–17, 168, 231
Mariposa Folk Festival, 44–5, *45*
Mattamy National Cycling Centre, 206–7, *207*
McCrae House, 210
McDougall Cottage, 215
McMaster Museum of Arts, 74
McMichael Canadian Art Collection,, 14–15, *15*
Mennonites, 230
Metcalf Rock, 62, *62*
mills, 149, 175–6
Milton, 206–7
Minesing Wetlands, 36–8, *36–7*
Mono Cliffs Provincial Park, 35
Montgomery, Lucy Maud, 140, *141*
Mosport Park, 147–9, *148–9*
motor sports, 147–9, 181
Mount St. Louis Moonstone, 67–8

Nancy Island Historic Site, 53
Nashville Conservation Reserve, 18
Nassagaweya Canyon Trail, 204
Niagara Escarpment, 81–5
Niagara Falls, 93–6, *94–6*, 99, 125
Niagara Freedom Trail, 123–5
Niagara Greenbelt Route, 100–1
Niagara River Recreation Trail, *98*, 99–100
Niagara wine region, 101, 107–11, *108*, *110*
Niagara-on-the-Lake (NOTL), 100, 112–17
Normandale, 119–20
North Beach Provincial Park, 188
Northumberland County, 166–9

Oak Ridges Moraine, 19–20, 139–42
Old Baldy Conservation Area, 66
Ontario Greenbelt, 150
Orangeville, 33–4
Orillia, 40–5, *41*, *43*
Orillia Farmers' Market, 40
Orillia Museum of Art and History, 42–3, *43*
Orono, 154
Oshawa, 132–4, 191–2

Palgrave Forest and Wildlife Area, 18
Paris, 216–19, *217*
Paris Museum & Historical Society, 218
Paris Surf, 219
parks and conservation areas, 17–22, 29, 35, 48–9, 66, 69, 169, 202–7
Parkwood National Historic Site, 134
Parliament Oak School, 124
Peterborough, 170–4
Peterborough Lift Lock, 172, *172*
Peter's Woods, 167–8, *167*
Picton, 184
Pigott Building, 78, *78*
pioneer village, 46–8, 175–6
Piping Plover, 54
Ploverpalooza, 54
Port Colborne, 92
Port Colborne Historical and Marine Museum, 92
Port Dover, 118–19
Port Dover Beach, 119
Port Dover Harbour Museum, 119
Port Hope, 156–61, *157, 158*
Port Hope House Tour, 159
Port Perry, 144–6
Port Ryerse, 119
powwows, 220–1
Presqu'ile Provincial Park, 178–80, *179*
Primitive Designs, 160–1, *161*
Prince Edward County (PEC), 182–90, *185*
Prince of Wales Hotel, *113*
printing press, 105–6, *106*

Queenston Heights, 102–6
Queenston Heights Park, 102–3, *102–3*

rafting/tubing, 216–17, *216*, 227, *227*
Rattlesnake Point, 203–4, *204*
Ravenna, 61–2
Ravenna Country Market, 61, *62*
Rice Lake, 177
Rice Lake Ramble, 164–5, *165*
Riverfest, 227
Robert McLaughlin Gallery, 132–4, *132–3*
Rock Garden, 80–1, *80*
rock-climbing, 204
Rogers House, 115–16
Rotary Greenway Trail, 173, *173*
Royal Botanical Gardens (RBG), 79–81
Royal George Theatre, *117*

Sainte-Marie among the Hurons, 46–8, *47*, *48*
Salem Chapel, 123–4
samosas, 202
Samuel de Champlain Monument, 42
Sandbanks Provincial Park, 188–9, *188*
Sandyford Place, 78
Scandinave Spa, 58, *58*
Scenic Caves, 58
Serpent Mounds, 177
Shakespearean Gardens, *234*
Sharon, 23–6
Sharon Burying Ground, 26, *26*
Shaw Festival, 114, 116–17
Shelburne, 33
Shelter Valley Cycling Route, 165
ships/boats, 49–50, 53, 88–7, 90–2, 95, 122, 172
Sifton-Cook Heritage Centre, 164
Simcoe, John Graves, 124
Simcoe Snowbelt, 67–9
Six Nations of the Grand River, 220–3
skating, 143–4
skiing, 34, 54, 55–61, 65, 67–9, 136, 138, 142, 153, 205–6
snowshoeing, 60–1, 154, 206
South Simcoe Railway, 34
St. Andrew's Presbyterian Church, 115, *115*
St. Catharines, 123
St. Jacobs, 228–32, *230*
St. Jacobs Antiques Market, 232
St. Jacobs Farmers' Market, 228–9, *229*
St. Jacobs Horse-Drawn Tours, 231, *231*
St. Mark's Anglican Church, *159*
steam engines, 88–9
Stillwaters Plate and Pour, 219, *219*
Stratford, 233–6
Stratford Festival, 233–5
Streets Alive! 43
swimming, 51–4

Temple of the Children of Peace, 23–6, *24*
Terra Cotta Conservation Area, 30–1, *31*
Terroir Spring Wine and Food Festival, 184
Tew Falls, 83, *83*, 84
Thomas Foster Memorial, 140–1, *141*
train rides, 34, 142, 164, 213, 231

Trans Canada Trail, 137–8
Treetop Trekking Ganaraska, 152
Trent University, 173, *173*
trilliums, 20, *20*
Tubman, Harriet, 124–5
Turkey Point, 120, 122
Tyrone Mills, 149–50, *149*

Underground Railroad, 92, 106–7, 113, 123–5
Uxbridge, 138
Uxbridge Township, 139–42
Uxbridge Trestle Bridge, 142, *142*

velodrome, 207
Victoria Hall, 163–4, *163*

Walker, James, 136
Walker Woods, 135–8
Warkworth, 168, *168*
Warsaw Caves Conservation Area, 174
Wasaga Beach, 51–4, 52, *54*
Wasaga Nordic Centre, 54
waterfalls, 66, 83–5, 93–6, 99, 125, 206
Waterloo Central Railway, 231
Webster Falls, 83–4, *83*
Welland Canal, 90–2, *90–2*
Wesleyville, 157
Wesleyville United Church, 157, *157*
West Montrose Covered Bridge, 232, *232*
Wilkies Bakery, 42, *42*
Willow Creek Canoe Corral, 37–8
Willowbank mansion, 104–5, *105*
Willson, David, 24–5, 26
wine tours, 109–11, 183–4
wineries, 101, 107–11, 182–4, 187–8
Winslow Farm, 177
Woodland Cultural Centre, 223
Wye Marsh Wildlife Centre, 48–9, *49*

York Durham Heritage Railway, 142

Zephyr, 140
zoos, 213–14